USE YOUR DREAMS TO DEVELOP YOUR NEXT BOOK, CREATIVE PROJECT, OR BUSINESS IDEA

by Gini Graham Scott, Ph.D.

USE YOUR DREAMS TO DEVELOP YOUR NEXT BOOK, CREATIVE PROJECT, OR BUSINESS IDEA

Copyright © 2018 by Gini Graham Scott

All rights reserved. No part of this book may be used or reproduced by any means, graphic, electronic, or mechanical, including photocopying, recording, taping or by any information storage retrieval system without the written permission of the author except in the case of brief quotations embodied in critical articles and reviews.

TABLE OF CONTENTS

INTRODUCTION 5
CHAPTER 1: HOW DREAMS HAVE INSPIRED NEW
PROJECTS AND SHAPED HISTORY 9
My Own Experience with Dreams and New Projects 10
Well-Known Dreams that Led to Breakthroughs 12
From Dreams to Books 12
The Inspiration for Films 14
Dreams and Music 15
Scientific Breakthroughs and Dreams 16
New Technologies, Inventions, and Businesses 20
What We Can Learn from Our Dreams 22
The Many Ways Dreams Have Been Used Throughout History 24
CHAPTER 2: HOW TO REMEMBER AND KEEP TRACK OF
YOUR DREAMS 29
Keep a Dream Journal, Notebook, or Recording Device by Your Bed
.... 30
Review What You Have Written or Recorded 32
CHAPTER 3: HOW TO UNDERSTAND AND APPLY THE
MEANING OF YOUR DREAMS 35
Common Reasons for Dreaming 36
Common Meanings in Dreams 40
Finding Your Own Meanings in Your Dreams 48
CHAPTER 4: USING YOUR DREAM TO BRAINSTORM NEW
IDEAS AND TURN THOSE IDEAS INTO A REALITY 49
Beginning the Brainstorming Process 50
Different Ways of Brainstorming 52
   Some Ways to Liberate the Creative Process 57
   Keeping Track of Your Ideas 62
CHAPTER 5: ASSESSING, PRIORITIZING, AND
IMPLEMENTING YOUR IDEAS 65
   Reviewing and Assessing Your Ideas 66
   Implementing Your New Ideas 70

CHAPTER 6: HOW TO DREAM MORE AND INFLUENCE YOUR DREAMS 73
   Set Aside Some Time When You Can Go to Sleep and Dream .. 74
   Encourage Yourself to Dream about a Particular Topic 75
   Use Lucid Dreaming to Guide Your Dream................................ 79
   Create a Dream Environment that Encourages You to Have More Dreams -- and More Productive Ones.. 83
   Drawing Insights from Other Types of Dreaming or Dreamlike States... 86
      Daydreaming... 86
      Relaxing 87
      Meditating... 88
      Hypnosis 89
   Summing Up.. 91
CHAPTER 7: TURN YOUR DREAM IDEAS INTO A NEW BOOK OR PROJECT 93
CHAPTER 8: CREATING A SUPPORT GROUP TO ENCOURAGE AND NUTURE YOUR DREAMS 97
ABOUT THE AUTHOR 101

INTRODUCTION

Dreams have had a long history of inspiring actions that have changed the world. They have inspired great scientific discoveries, symphonies, art works, political actions, and the outcomes of wars. Psychiatrists from Freud on have used dreams to gain insights into what their patients are really feeling about something.

You can likewise use your dreams to help you create books, other creative projects, and new business ventures. You can shape your dreams to answer questions and lead to new insights. Or learn to pay attention to your random dreams and mine them for guidance on what to do. You can learn to remember your dreams more, so they are there to guide you.

I began thinking about dreams after I had a dream that stayed with me, although most of my dreams have faded soon after waking. Sometimes they are gone right away, though I know I have dreamt about something, but the content is elusive, never to be pulled out of the subconscious, that is like a like a lake for drowned thoughts and dreams.

However, in this case, the dream stayed with me, perhaps inspired by my efforts earlier that day to sign up for a dinner and movie on New Year's Eve. I had s planned to go to relax after several days of working too hard.

Then I had my dream that night. In my dream, I was going to meet a group of people in a field near my house to go to a film. But when I got to the meeting place, only a handful of people were gathered at a picnic table and others hadn't arrived yet. As we waited and no one else arrived, I realized I had forgotten my ticket. So I went back to my house to get my ticket. When I returned 5 or 10 minutes later, a few more people were at the table, but the group was still waiting for more arrivals.

But now I realized I didn't have my wallet, which must be back at my house. I told everyone I needed to go back for it and would return soon, so please wait for me. However, my house now seemed further away, so it took longer to walk there, and I worried that people might leave before I got back. And that's exactly what happened. When I got back, no one was at the picnic table.

So where did they go? At first I thought I could meet them at the movie theater. But I couldn't remember which one it was. I tried thinking of different possibilities and woke up feeling lost.

After that, the dream was so intense that I remembered it, as if I was asking me to pay attention to what it was trying to tell me. At first, I wondered if I really wanted to go to this event, because I had other things to do instead.

Then as I thought more about the power of dreams to influence and inspire us, I realized this other thing to do was develop this book -- how dreams can lead us to our next book, creative project, or business venture.

So that became the mission triggered by this dream -- if you pay attention to your dreams, they can guide you on what to do next in your work and your life.

To illustrate, the book covers these key topics:
- How dreams have inspired many creative projects and decisions that have changed the world;
- Remembering and keeping track of your dreams by writing them down and collecting them in a dream diary or journal;

- Understanding the meaning of your dreams, relating them to daily life, and getting inspiration from them.
- Using the dream to brainstorm new ideas and turning those ideas into a reality
- Dreaming more and guiding your dreams by using lucid dreaming and triggering dreams before you go to bed.

- Creating a dream environment that encourages more dreaming and a positive dream experience.
- Drawing insights from other types of dreaming -- such as from daydreaming or inspirations while meditating, or relaxing and letting the ideas flow in.
- Shaping your book based on your ideas from a dream: what is the big idea, who is book for, and creating an outline.
- Turning your dreams into a new project by clarifying what this is, determining who might want it, creating a prototype or working model, and testing out whether this works or what others think about it.
- Sharing your dreams with others by creating a support group that encourages dreaming, getting ideas from your dreams, and implementing the best ideas.

CHAPTER 1: HOW DREAMS HAVE INSPIRED NEW PROJECTS AND SHAPED HISTORY

Many well-known books, films, musical works, scientific projects, inventions, business innovations, and other developments that have shaped our society have been inspired by dreams. And if others can turn their dreams into creative projects or ideas for business ventures, so can you -- whether it's a book, piece of art, business or other idea. You just have to pay attention to your dreams and cultivate your ability to dream and remember your dreams.

First, for inspiration, here are examples of some well-known dreams that have resulted in breakthroughs in different fields. Often you will see these dreams listed together, usually by the numbers, such as:

- "10 Dreams that Changed Human History" by Rebecca Turner with the World-of-Lucid-Dreaming.Com,
- "Twelve Famous Dreams: Creativity and Famous Discoveries From Dreams," from Brilliant Dreams.com,
- 11 Creative Breakthroughs People Had in Their Sleep" by Stacy Conradt writing in *Mental Floss*,
- "25 Dreams that Forever Changed Society" by Alex Salamanca on List25.com.

I have organized them by category, so you can see the way dreams have had a big influence in a wide variety of fields. In general, these dreams have come to people who are already involved in that field and often have already achieved some prominence. But then they have come up against some creative block where the dream provides an answer, or the dream leads them to create something novel in their field.

Thus, the dream commonly results from something someone is already thinking about; then the dream provides a new twist on that thinking that leads to breakthrough results, perhaps because the dream comes from the person's subconscious or unconscious, so it is not hemmed in by more linear analytical thinking. Instead, it provides a holistic, intuitive vision that leads to new thinking.

My Own Experience with Dreams and New Projects

I had this experience myself many times. For example, soon after I started a games club in my twenties, a friend who had recently learned about hypnosis used this technique to lead me to Macy's department store while I was in a relaxed state. He asked me to imagine going down in an elevator to Macy's basement where I could see all kinds of toys. Among them I could see many new toys that were never developed before. I don't remember what I saw there, just a lot of shelves. But a few nights later I had a dream that led to my first published game. I saw a bunch of screws and the circles chasing each other around a board. Along the way, some of the pieces caught up to each other, and the circles jumped onto the screws or the screws pulled the circles on top of them. The result was a board game called *Oh Peg It!*, where players moved screws and circles around a circular board like a race track, and the idea was to see who could peg the most for the highest score. And sometimes players acquired cards with funny slogans, such as "Go peg yourself," or "A peg in time saves nine." Within a few weeks I made a prototype of the game, and a few months later, I sold it to a small game company in San Diego.

A few years later, another dream led me to visualize a large ball with screws of different sizes put through it, which led to a puzzle based on taking out all the screws and putting them back, so they all fit. To make a prototype for the puzzle, I went to a hardware store, where I bought some 4" to 5" long bolts, and then I found some clear plastic spheres made of two halves that snap together. Eventually, this turned into a puzzle called *Screwball* that I sold to Hasbro Industries, which was then and still is one of the major toy companies.

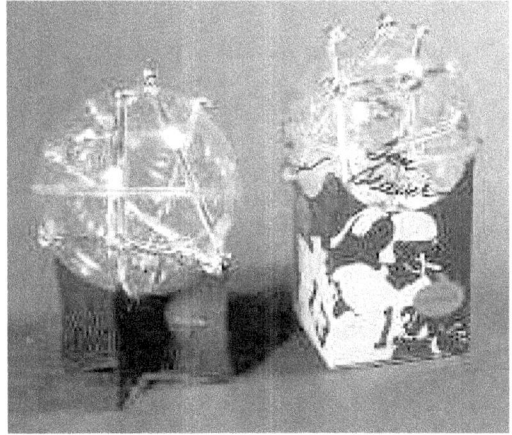

Since then, after I turned to writing books and scripts, I got many of my ideas for these from my dreams, just like the many well-known dreamers in history. Here are their famous breakthrough dreams, organized by their fields of endeavor.

Well-Known Dreams that Led to Breakthroughs

While dreams have inspired all types of projects, the most well-known ones are in these major categories: books, films, music, science, technology, inventions, and business.

From Dreams to Books

<u>The Creation of Frankenstein</u>. Yes, good old Frankenstein began as a dream, which Mary Shelley had in 1916, leading her to create what is often called "the world's first science fiction novel." As the story goes in numerous accounts, when she was 18 or 19, she visited Lord Byron in Switzerland one winter, and during the cold nights, they were stuck indoors and got to talking about writing ghost stories and the nature of life. Shelly suggested that a corpse could be reanimated based on galvanism, the then popular notion that a chemical action could produce electricity and that a muscle stimulated by electricity could contract. Later that night, Shelley experienced a vivid waking dream in which a man who studied the "unhallowed arts" had put together a corpse of a man and stimulated it into life. The dream frightened her, though it inspired the beginnings of her ghost story, and in the morning she announced to the gathering that the dream had led to this idea. And the rest, as they say, is history.[1]

<u>The Story of Dr. Jekyll and Mr. Hyde</u>. This is another literary classic that began as a dream. In this case, Robert Louis Stevenson had been trying to come up with a plot for a novel, when he had a

---

[1] Rebecca Turner, "10 Dreams that Changed History," World of Lucid Dreaming, www.world-of-lucid-dreaming-com/10-dreams-that-chagned-the-course-of-human-history.html

dream in which a man being pursued for a crime took a powder and underwent a change in his being in front of his pursuers. Inspired by this dream, he wrote and printed the book within 10 weeks. In fact, this dream was one of many dreams which Stevenson had that inspired his writing, since from an early age, his vivid dreams inspired many stories. Early on, Stevenson found that he was able to dream complete stories, and he could even return to a dream to come up with a different ending. And later in life, he trained himself to remember his dreams and use them to develop plots for his books.[2]

<u>The Creation of Twilight.</u>   Still another horror tale, the *Twilight* series by Stephanie Meyer, began with a dream. In this case, Meyer had a vivid dream in which a "beautiful, sparkly boy" who was a vampire and a girl who was a normal human being were on a bright sunny meadow having a conversation in which the boy tried to explain to the girl how much he cared for her yet wanted to kill her. In the morning, Meyer wrote the dream down in order to remember it, because it was so different from her normal life as a stay-at-home mom. And eventually that provided the basis for her novel that turned into a series later filmed with Robert Pattison and Kristen Stewart.[3]

---

[2] "Twelve Famous Dreams: Creativity and Famous Discoveries from Dreams," Brilliant Dreams, www.brilliantdreams.com/product/famous-dreams.htm
[3] Stacy Conradt, "11 Creative Breakthroughs People Had in Their Sleep," *Mental Floss,* October 11, 2012, http://mentalfloss.com/article/12763/11-creative-breakthroughs-people-had-in-their-sleep

<u>The Inspiration for Stephen King's *Misery*.</u> This is one more nightmare that later turned to gold for an author. In this case, Stephen King had his dream on an airplane in which a women held a writer prisoner, killed him, skinned him, fed the remains to her pig, and bound his novel in human skin. Eventually, this became the best-selling novel and later film *Misery*, thought the plot changed a little in the course of writing it. As the novel goes, a bestselling novelist has a car accident leading him to meet his number one fan, who nurses him back to health. But she is also angry that he has killed off her favorite character in his latest book, so she keeps him a captive prisoner in her isolated house. She wants him to write a book that brings Misery back to life just for her, and she spurs him on with various tortures, including a needle, axe, and even more.[4]

The Inspiration for Films

<u>James Cameron's Terminator.</u>   One of the most famous film monsters also came from a dream, the *Terminator*, well-known for Arnold Schwarzenegger as the robot and his famous line: "I'll be back." The story was originally inspired by James Cameron, sick with a fever of 102 degrees, having a nightmare in which he saw a metallic figure with piercing red eyes pulling itself out of a fire. So that was the basis for this robot, who in the story is a cyborg assassin sent back in time from 2029 to 1984 to kill a woman whose son will become a savior against machines in a post-apocalyptic future.[5] Eventually, this film was so successful that it led to five sequels -- the 6th film in the series to be released in 2019. And it all started with a dream.

---

[4] Stacy Conradt, "11 Creative Breakthroughs People Had in Their Sleep," *Mental Floss,* October 11, 2012, http://mentalfloss.com/article/12763/11-creative-breakthroughs-people-had-in-their-sleep
[5] Alex Salamanca, "25 Dreams that Forever Changed Society," *People and Politics,* May 20, 2015. https://list25.com/25-dreams-that-forever-changed-society

Dreams and Music

Dreams have also inspired a number of music numbers. Among them:

The Beatle's Song *Yesterday* came to Paul McCartney in a dream in 1965. He woke up hearing the music in his head and wrote it out on a piano. Later, he and John Lennon recorded the song, and it became a number one song on the Billlboard Hot 100 Chart for four weeks. In fact, it is still popular today. Over 2200 cover versions have been released by well- known artists, including Katy Perry, Bob Dylan, Elvis Presley and Michael Bolton.[6]

The Rolling Stone's *(I Can't Get No) Satisfaction* resulted from Keith Richard's dream. In it, he imagined the acoustic riffs and jotted them down before falling back to sleep.[7]

---

[6] Rebecca Turner, "10 Dreams that Changed History," World of Lucid Dreaming, www.world-of-lucid-dreaming-com/10-dreams-that-chagned-the-course-of-human-history.html

[7] Alex Salamanca, "25 Dreams that Forever Changed Society," *People and Politics,* May 20, 2015. https://list25.com/25-dreams-that-forever-changed-society

Beethoven's Many Piano Sonatas. Supposedly, Beethoven heard many of his sonatas in his dreams and wrote them down. According to some historians, he even dreamt of instruments not yet invented. [8]

George Frederic Handel's Messiah. In this case, Handel's dreams came to the rescue when he couldn't figure out an ending to the Messiah, and the ending came to him in a dream. [9]

Scientific Breakthroughs and Dreams

Science has been an especially fertile field for dreams, with many breakthroughs by scientists attributed to dreams. These include:

- *The Chemical Transmission of Nerve Impulses by Dr. Otto Loewi,* a German born physiologist who won the Nobel Prize in medicine in 1936 for his work on this subject. The inspiration for his dream traces back to 1903, when he first thought that nervous impulses might be transmitted chemically rather than by an electrical impulse, as commonly believed. But Loewi wasn't sure how to prove this, until he had a dream in 1920 about how to conduct an experiment to do this. He then performed an experiment on a frog's heart which worked, and over the next decade he carried out other tests to show his idea was right.[10]

- *The Discovery of the Structure of Carbon and the Benzene Molecule by Friedrich August Kekule,* While Kekule had a long career in organic chemistry, he made some of his most notable achievements as a result of some dreams, not just by experimenting alone. In one dream, which inspired the structural theory of matter, he saw small atoms dancing around. He had seen the atoms in

---

[8] Salamanca.
[9] Salamanca.
[10] "Twelve Famous Dreams: Creativity and Famous Discoveries from Dreams," Brilliant Dreams, www.brilliantdreams.com/product/famous-dreams.htm.

motion before, but now he saw two smaller atoms unite to form a pair, while larger atoms embraced the two smaller ones. Then, even larger atoms held on to three or four smaller ones. After that, Kekule saw the larger ones form a chain, where they dragged the smaller onto the end of the chain. After he woke up, he drew sketches of these dream forms which led him to create the Structure Theory. Later, a dream, which has become very famous, led him to discover that the benzene molecule, which unlike other organic compounds, had a circular structure rather than a linear one. In this dream, he saw the atoms gamboling about as before, but this time long rows of atoms twisted and twined together like the movement of a snake. Then, he saw one of the snakes grab its own tail, and this image was the source of the circular structure idea that helped him solve the problem of the benzene molecule.[11]

---

[11]"Twelve Famous Dreams: Creativity and Famous Discoveries from Dreams," Brilliant Dreams, www.brilliantdreams.com/product/famous-dreams.htm.

<u>The Periodic Table by Dmitry Mendeleyev</u>. This science breakthrough from a dream occurred in 1869 when Mendeleyev was preparing the definitive textbook of the day: *Principles of Chemistry*. After working for three straight days, he had a dream about arranging the elements into a table, where all of the elements fell into their proper place on the chart. He arranged the 63 elements then known so that all the physical and chemical properties of an element with similar properties were in a vertical column on the table. As soon as he awoke, he wrote down the results.[12]

<u>The Shape and Structure of DNA by Dr. James Watson.</u> He saw this image in a dream in 1953. Until then, scientists hadn't figured out DNA's shape or structure, but Watson dreamt about two intertwined serpents with heads at either end, or maybe he dreamt of a spiral staircase, according to some accounts. In either case, his dream showed the twisted intertwined nature of DNA.[13]

<u>The Structure of the Atom by Niels Bohr</u>. In this case, Bohr, a noted physicist and the father of quantum mechanics, was struggling with trying to understand the structure of the atom in 1913, but none of his designs worked. Then, he had a dream in which he saw electrons spinning around the nucleus of the atom, much like planets spin around the sun. It was truly an eureka moment, though Bohr returned to the lab to seek evidence to support his vision, which it did, leading to a breakthrough in physics. Later, Bohr won the 1922 Nobel Prize for Physics for his basic understanding of the atom.[14]

<u>The Speed of Light by Albert Einstein.</u> Even Einstein's great achievement of discovering the principle of relativity was

---

[12] "Creative Breakthroughs People Had in Their Sleep," http://mentalfloss.com/article/12763/11-creative-breakthroughs-people-had-in-their-sleep

[13] "Creative Breakthroughs People Had in Their Sleep.

[14] Rebecca Turner, "10 Dreams that Changed History," World of Lucid Dreaming, www.world-of-lucid-dreaming-com/10-dreams-that-chagned-the-course-of-human-history.html

inspired by a dream. In his dream, he was sledding so fast down a steep mountainside that he approached the speed of light. As he did so, the stars in his dream changed their appearance, and when he woke up, he thought about this idea and soon came up with his famous E=mc2 theory.[15]

 The Notion of Infinity by Srinvasa Ramanujan. A famous mathematician who developed over 3000 mathematical theorems in his lifetime, Ramanujan got many of his insights from his dreams. Among other things, he contributed ideas about the analytical theory of numbers, elliptical functions, continued fractions, and infinite series, many inspired by his dreams. Ramanujan said the Hindu goddess Namakkal came to him again and again and gave him complex mathematical formulas. He then sought to test them out after he woke up to see if they were true. One such dream was for the infinite series for Pi.[16]

---

[15] http://www.dreaminterpretation-dictionary.com/famous-dreams-albert-einstein.html
[16] Rebecca Turner, "10 Dreams that Changed History," World of Lucid Dreaming, www.world-of-lucid-dreaming-com/10-dreams-that-chagned-the-course-of-human-history.html

<u>A Medical Cure for Diabetes by Frederick Banting.</u> Still another Nobel Prize winner, Banting, was inspired by a dream in 1921. Then a surgeon with a BA in medicine, Banting was working with a colleague, Dr. Charles Best, to find the cure for diabetes after his mother died of this disease. He thought the secretion of pancreatic juices could be harmful to the secretions of the pancreas, and he had a dream which told him to tie up the pancreas of a dog to stop the flow of nourishment. When Banting tied it up, he found an imbalance between sugar and insulin. Then, he had another dream about how to treat diabetes with insulin, and after some experiments proved this method worked, he gained the Nobel Prize for this discovery in 1923.[17]

New Technologies, Inventions, and Businesses

Finally, dreams have led to inventions and technologies that have contributed to new businesses and industries, much like my dreams inspired games that were published by major companies. Some dreams about new technologies, inventions, and business ventures are these.

<u>The Invention of the Sewing Machine by Elias Howe.</u> In 1845, Howe already had the idea of a sewing machine, in which a needle would go through a piece of cloth. But he had trouble getting the machine to work. He had already tried and failed using a needle with an eye in the middle. Then, one night, in a dream, a group of natives took him prisoner and danced around him with spears. As they danced, he noticed that the spears had holes near their tips, and he woke up realizing that spear image solved his problem. He could locate the hole at the tip of the needle rather than in the middle, and in the morning, he created a model of such a machine with the eye at the point of the needle. Now the needle could catch the thread after it went through the machine, so the machine finally worked. This

---

[17] Turner.

discovery was the basis for the Singer Sewing Machine company, which turned the sewing machine into an everyday household item.[18]

 The Dream Development of Google by Larry Page. Even Google was born from a dream. That occurred when Larry Page was working with an academic mentor, Terry A. Winograd, a computer science professor who won a National Science Foundation grant to examine the future development of online information. One night Larry had a vivid dream in which he saw that it might be possible download the whole web onto computers, and use links to connect one website to another. This idea then led to the development of a search engine that would use these links to catalog the whole worldwide web. After Page told his friend Sergey Brin about the idea, the two began developing the idea, and now the web Google created is everywhere.[19]

---

[18]"Twelve Famous Dreams: Creativity and Famous Discoveries from Dreams."
[19] Mick Gibson, "The Dream that Lead to Google," MickG, May 31, 2010. http://www.mickg.com.au/the-dream-that-lead-to-google.

<u>A Dream that Created a Cosmetics Company and Created the First Female Self-Made Millionaire, Madame C. J. Walker.</u> To take one more example, a dream led Madame Walker to found a cosmetic company that was a milestone, since she was the first member of her family to be born free, and the cosmetics idea from her dream resulted in her becoming a multi-millionaire, a first for a female black American. The dream came to her in 1890 after she was suffering from a scalp infection that led her to lose most of her hair. To stop the infection, she began experimenting with patented medicines and hair care products, but nothing seemed to work. Then, one night in a dream, a big black man appeared to her and told her what to mix for her hair, using many plants grown in Africa. After she ordered the remedy, mixed it, and put it on her scalp, it worked. Soon her hair was growing faster than it was falling out, and when she tried the mixture on her friends, it helped them, too. So from working in the cotton fields and a kitchen, she began manufacturing hair preparations and built her own factory, which turned her into a millionaire. She was even honored on a U.S. postal stamp.[20]

What We Can Learn from Our Dreams

These dreams about creative projects -- from books and films to breakthroughs in science, technology, and business -- show the power of dreams to inspire new ideas, though such dreams do not come randomly. Rather, they are triggered by what one is already working on or thinking about, especially if one has encountered a barrier or problem. Then, the dream extends that thinking into new realms and provides a creative twist that enables the dreamer to find a new solution, like seeing the snake grabbing its tail to show how to design the benzene molecule, or seeing a monster to suggest a new ghost story in Mary Shelley's case.

These dreams often come when one is very tired after a long night of thinking about something, so one has reached an impasse

---

[20] Twelve Famous Dreams: Creativity and Famous Discoveries from Dreams," Brilliant Dreams, www.brilliantdreams.com/product/famous-dreams.htm.

and falls asleep feeling stuck. Then, the dream leads to a refreshed take on the subject.

Such dreams are often very vivid, so they draw attention and are memorable. They don't quickly fade away but get the person, now awake, to experience the dream's power. Often that means thinking about the meaning of the dream or what action the dream seems to be demanding. Notably, many of these creative dreamers quickly write down the dream and use what they have written to guide action. This doesn't mean they exactly follow the details of the dream. For example, after a dream led Stephen King to write *Misery*, he changed some of the plot elements, as did James Cameron in turning his dream into *The Terminator*.

Notably, many of the dreams for creative projects come from nightmares, especially the dreams leading to plots for books and films. Such dreams are tapping into fears and other dark emotions that many people have but are afraid to express openly. They may not even want to acknowledge those feelings. Yet the dreams bring out such fears, which sometimes take the form of monsters, demons, and otherworldly beings. So no wonder those creative projects are so compelling, because they provide a way to express hidden urges and taboos, and they provide an acceptable way of showing the universality of these feelings.

Thus, the dream becomes a kind of creative spark to turn on one's creative engine. It is like the fuel that drives the car, but the driver steers it. It provides the inspiration to do something great, but you have to turn that inspiration into action in your field, whether that means writing, creating a prototype, or building a business. For example, many scientists used their dreams to envision a solution in their research, but afterwards they had to engage in numerous experiments to prove the idea suggested by their dream.

These individuals who used their dreams to inspire breakthroughs in their work didn't specifically look to their dreams for answers. Rather, the dreams seemed to come to them at a time when they needed that idea. But you can proactively trigger these dreams. Beyond just paying attention and getting insights from your dreams, you can learn to better access them and guide the dreaming process in a certain direction. This way, you can learn even more and gain further insights from your dreams. As such, you will be joining a long history of individuals and cultures using dreams for many purposes.

The Many Ways Dreams Have Been Used Throughout History

The use of dreams to shape one's personal life and lead others goes back at least 5000 years ago to 3100 BC, when the Sumerians in Mesopotamia believed the dreamer left his body while sleeping in order to travel to a dream world, and the Sumerian kings recorded their dreams on clay tablets. A little later, the Babylonians and Assyrians divided dreams into good and bad dreams, sent respectively by the gods or demons, and they believed their dreams could predict future events through prophesies or omens.[21]

In 2000 BC, dreams became even more influential. As Amy Cope describes in the "History of Dreams," the Egyptians wrote down their dreams on papyrus, and they especially valued one's

---

[21] Amy Cope, "History of Dreams," Dreams into Life, http://amycope.com/history-of-dreams

ability to have very vivid or significant dreams. They even placed such a high value on dreams that they built temples devoted to dreaming. They believed that if a sick person went to sleep in a dream temple, those individuals would receive messages from the gods in their dreams to help them heal. The Egyptians even had priests who served as dream interpreters by helping the people in the temples interpret their dreams.[22]

Later, the Ancient Greeks drew on the ideas about dreaming from the Egyptians. Among other things, they believed that the gods and goddesses, or the dead, sent messages through dreams, and that dreams could predict the future, provide solutions to problems, and help them decide what actions to take. In fact, Greek military and political leaders looked to dream interpreters to help them make military and political decisions.[23]

And the Bible includes many stories people getting messages and visions from God in their dreams in the form of symbols to interpret or direct instructions about what to do. For example, author Jeffrey Kranz reports that there are 21 dreams recorded in the Bible. In one dream, God tells Abimelech, the king of Gerar, to avoid sleeping with Sarah, Abraham's wife, since she is not Abraham's sister, as he was told incorrectly. In another well-known dream, Jacob climbs a ladder from Earth to heaven, where God tells Jacob that He will give the land where he is now staying to him and his descendants. In another dream, God appears to Solomon, the new king of Israel, and offers to give him whatever he wants, whereupon Solomon chooses wisdom. Later, in the New Testament, in a dream, an angel tells Joseph, the carpenter, not to divorce Mary, and she later gives birth to Jesus. In another dream, an angel tells Joseph to escape before Herold slaughters all male babies.[24]

The Native Americans, too, placed a great value in dreaming, since they believed the dream world was an alternate reality and

---

[22] "Twelve Famous Dreams: Creativity and Famous Discoveries from Dreams," Brilliant Dreams, www.brilliantdreams.com/product/famous-dreams.htm.
[23] Amy Cope.
[24] Jeffrey Kranz, "Infographic: Every Dream in the Bible (and What They Mean), Overview Bible, October 16, 2017, http://overviewbible.com/infographic-dreams-bible

messages from dreams provided very valuable information, such as guidance for rituals and medicines. Among some tribes, youths entering puberty would be sent on a vision quest, where they would stay alone in the forest and fast for days, until they had a dream or vision about themselves and their place in the tribe.[25]

More recently, the ideas of Sigmund Freud and Carl Jung have influenced modern psychology and psychiatry based on interpreting dreams to help patients overcome psychological problems and early childhood traumas. While Freud emphasized looking to dreams to recognize sexual urges, wishes, and fears and gain insights into previous emotional traumas to heal, Jung had a more positive spin on the value of understanding dreams. Among other things, he believed that dreams provided insights into our unconscious desires, wishes, and forgotten pieces of ourselves. He considered dreams to be messages, and we should pay attention to them and act on this information from our subconscious mind to live a more fulfilling life.[26]

---

[25] Amy Cope, "History of Dreams," Dreams into Life, http://amycope.com/history-of-dreams
[26] Amy Cope

The focus of this book is on looking to your dreams to develop creative projects, such as books, new technologies, and successful businesses. At the same time, you may gain insights about yourself and what to do for your personal growth and healing. If so, use whatever messages you get from your dreams to not only create profitable projects but to gain more self-understanding and personal guidance.

CHAPTER 2: HOW TO REMEMBER AND KEEP TRACK OF YOUR DREAMS

A first step to paying attention to your dreams and remembering them is writing them down or recording them as soon after you have a dream as possible. Once you start making a record of your dreams, you will have more dreams with more details, because you are giving your dreams this extra attention.

Even if you don't look at what you have written or recorded immediately, you will still have a record of each dream you can readily look back to, when you are ready to turn the message of your dream into something tangible. I have been writing down my own dreams for over 30-years. Sometimes I look back on them for insights on what I have done and what I might do now with this dream information. And sometimes I immediately put a dream into action.

There are a number of ways to keep track of your dreams.

Keep a Dream Journal, Notebook, or Recording Device by Your Bed

It can be easy to forget your dreams if you don't quickly record your experience and fall asleep again or get busy with the events of the day. Later, when you try to remember, you might only remember snips and can't remember the rest. Or sometimes all you might remember is you had a dream, but you can't recall what it was about. Or perhaps you may not think you had a dream, though sometimes during the day some image or incident triggers your recall, so some or most of the dream comes back. But you could have probably remembered much more had you recorded your experience at the time.

You can record your experience in any number of ways:

- Keep a dream journal in a book for dreams. You can get books for this purpose in a gift shop or office supply store with a variety of covers -- from plain black vinyl to colorful cloth binding.

- Write down your dreams in a notebook with rings, so you can add pages as you write more.

- Use a clipboard with loose sheets of paper and later transfer them to a notebook or binder of notes.

- Recount your dreams into a recording device. Later, transcribe your files and add them to your notebook, so you can easily refer back to them. Otherwise, as you accumulate recordings, it can be hard to listen back because of the long time required, whereas you can readily flip from page to page with written notes.

- Make a sketch of whatever you have seen in your dream, such as an image of a person, animal, scene, words, or diagrams.

- Write up your recollections in a Word document or notepad on your computer or mobile device, or later type out your handwritten notes into a document.

- Or use a combination of methods.

Keep a dream journal, notebook, clipboard, or recording device by your bed or wherever else you go to sleep, so you can easily record your dream immediately upon waking. This way you can more readily go back to sleep if you wake up from the dream in the middle of the night. Or if you wake up and don't expect to go back to sleep, it's fine to go to your computer to type out your notes. I have kept my dream notes in all kinds of ways, except for speaking into a recording device, since I prefer writing. At one time, I mainly recorded my recollections in a journal, notebook, or on loose sheets of paper which I added to a notebook, although now I mostly write on my computer.

At times you may have an especially vivid dream, wake up in the middle of the night, and think you will remember your dream later, since it was so dramatic. So you go back to sleep, expecting to record it later. But as I have found, much of the time, you won't remember your dream, only pieces of it, or you might only remember you had a dream, but now you can't recall it. So it's best to record your recollections while still fresh in your mind, even as you fight off the urge to go back to sleep. Or at least make a few notes about the main events in your dream in the hopes they might trigger your memory later.

What if you don't remember or want to remember more? There are techniques to trigger another dream where you can dream again about what you previously dreamt about.

Review What You Have Written or Recorded

Once you have written or recorded your dream, feel free to go back to sleep if you are still tired and want to sleep some more.

Later, whenever you are ready, take a short time to review your written or spoken recording. This will help you remember that dream, as well as notice any insights to be gained from it. While some insights might suggest creative ideas to develop, others may be insights about yourself or advice to apply in your daily life. Either is useful information, though you can separate the dreams that suggest future creative projects from the others about yourself and your everyday life. For future reference, you can separate these ideas into different notebooks or dream collections, or you can mark them up in a single written record to categorize them, such as by using an initial to refer to different types. For instance, these types might be:
- a creative project in general ("CP"),
- a book ("B")
- a film idea ("F")
- an invention ("I")
- a new business venture ("V")
- personal development advice ("PD").

Often, you will get ideas to file away for future reference, but sometimes you may get an idea for something that inspires immediate action. If so, go ahead and implement the idea now, while the dream is very fresh in your memory, or to cite the old saying: "Strike while the iron is hot."

That's what I did with my game ideas. Soon after I woke up, with the dream fresh in my mind, I sketched out a board for the *Oh Peg It!* game and the *Screwball* puzzle, a round ball with bolts in it. And with some more recent dreams about book ideas, I wrote up an outline and started researching and writing up the chapters of the book, such as I have been doing with my dream about creating a book on learning from dream ideas.

It can be easy to later look at your recorded dream ideas and think, "Oh, what an interesting idea. I'll have to do something about that sometime." But if you really want something to come of that idea, act on it now -- or as soon as possible, which is what these individuals with these famous dreams that became breakthrough projects did.

So if you think your dream suggests a good idea for a project, start thinking as quickly as you can about how you can turn that into a reality. Or if your dream suggests helpful advice to apply in your own life, think about how to implement that advice now.

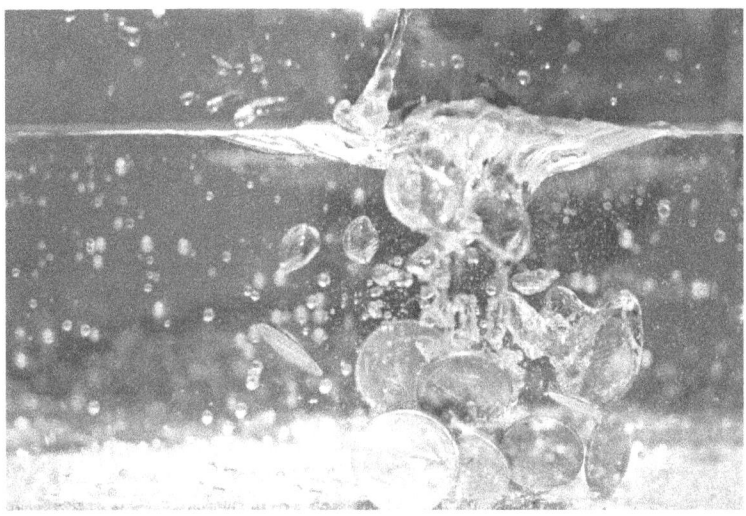

The process is much like what to do to achieve any goal. You outline the steps to get to that goal. You record what to do to implement those steps, such as acquiring the needed materials, people, or funds to make it happen. And you set up a timeline for what to do when. The big difference is you are starting with insights and suggestions from a dream. Otherwise the process of setting and making that goal happen is the same.

Sometimes, the meaning for what to do can be very clear in the dream itself. You see the plot for a novel or film, the key points for a self-help or business book; the way to design an invention, the product or service for a new business. But at other times, you just get some dream fragments, images, or events that aren't very clear, so you aren't sure what it all means. That's when you need some help in interpreting the meaning of your dreams and relating them to your daily life or business. That's what I'll talk about next.

CHAPTER 3: HOW TO UNDERSTAND AND APPLY THE MEANING OF YOUR DREAMS

Not every dream is the source of ideas for creative projects, so look for dreams that are relevant and think about how you can apply them. Sometimes the meanings hidden in dreams can give you ideas, so consider those as well in determining if your dream is relevant.

What's important is what the dream means to you, after you pay attention and remember it, though there are all sorts of guides that suggest common meanings or reasons for dreams. Sometimes these guides can help you to think about dreams, but often they are not relevant, since they are drawn from common meanings suggested by psychologists, researchers, and others. Moreover, most of these interpretations are designed to help you improve your personal life and recognize fears and barriers holding you back; they are not focused on gaining insights to stimulate your thinking about new projects or finding answers to overcome challenge in designing or implementing these projects.

Common Reasons for Dreaming

This search for meanings for dreams and how to apply them has a long history. Early on, dream interpreters viewed dreams as a way to make decisions for major undertakings. For example, seers trained to understand dreams helped Egyptian leaders interpret their dreams to plan battles and make state decisions, while the ancient Greeks and Romans thought that some dreams were predictions and premonitions of future events.

More recently, psychologists and psychiatrists starting with Freud have looked for more personal reasons, such as Freud's view that dreams express one's repressed conflicts or desires.[27] Now psychologists and neurologists use imaging equipment, such as PET scans and MRIs, to analyze the operations of the brain while one is dreaming. Among other things, they speculate that the brain uses dreaming to dump excess data, consolidate important information, and alert us to danger.[28] Plus dreaming can be a source of insights and ideas for creative and profitable projects.

---

[27] Jeffrey Kluger, "What Your Dreams Actually Mean, According to Science," *Time,* September 12, 2017. http://time.com/4921605/dreams-meaning
[28] Ibid.

As a data dump, researchers suggest that the brain uses a dream to get rid of useless memories from the day and cache valuable ones. Supposedly, the neocortex fires during sleep to send signals to various regions of the hippocampus to clear out whatever information it is holding in short-term storage, so it can gather more memory data the next day. The neocortex decides what data to discard. Then, as the data streams by in your mind which operates like a computer, some of this information is randomly picked up and turned into dreams. But whether or not the process is happening, you can look on whatever information comes through as fodder for your insights and ideas.

Moreover, this information can readily become organized data, since many dream theorists suggest that during information processing, our dreams sort information into categories, compare them to other events, and incorporate other information that we would otherwise suppress during the day.[29] Thus, this is another reason why dreams can be a source for new ideas by giving us a new take on our experiences and any information we have obtained each day.

As for the alert about potential future danger, that alert can suggest ideas for new projects, too, if we think about these dangers as problems to be solved. As Jeffrey Kluger points out in his *Time* article: "What Dreams Actually Mean, According to Science," Antti Revonsuo, a cognitive neuroscientist, of Sweden's University of Skovde, has proposed the Threat Simulation Theory whereby the brain responds to the perception of possible future danger by creating wake-up calls in the form of "fire drills" while we sleep, so we stay alert and sharp and are therefore ready to react as needed.[30]

For instance, if you dream about failing to pass a test, that could represent your fear about not being able to measure up in performing some task at work. At the same time, that dream could serve as a reminder to do some personal work, so you are more prepared in the future. Or you can look on such a warning as information that could be turned into a profitable project in your

---

[29]Kluger.
[30] Ibid.

field. For example, an engineer might find that a dream suggests a need for a better performance monitoring device to chart one's daily progress. A computer programmer might consider creating an app to guide users in what to do each day. Or a writer might find inspiration in a dream about failure on a test to write a self-help book on how to stay on task or a business book about how a manager can help a team's performance. In other words, if you think about your dream for insights into a new project, that awareness can give you useful ideas you can further develop.

Then, too, researchers have found that our dreams are often a means of problem solving in that many dreams draw on work we were doing during the day, but our waking mind encountered some problem or challenge we couldn't resolve. Yet, the dream can often resolve it, because the dream considers the problem from a more holistic or intuitive perspective to contribute a solution or scientific breakthroughs, such as a dream providing the solution to Kekule's benzene molecule by showing a snake grabbing its tail to suggest a circular structure rather than a linear one.

Likewise, if you are attuned to your dreams, you can apply them to current problems and even turn the solutions into products for others with similar problems. You can also take steps to more often have such problem solving dreams. Often such dreams occur randomly after you have been stumped by a particular difficulty, though at other times, you don't dream about the problem at all. However, by priming the pump with suggestions on what to dream about before you go to sleep for the night or take a nap, such a dream might suggest answers to your problem.

Finally, another reason for dreaming is wish-fulfillment. You have a dream about something you would like to do. Say you have a dream about flying; that could reflect a desire for more freedom in your life -- or it may simply mean you would like to take a vacation somewhere. Or if you dream about a new house, that could mean you want more opportunity or novelty in your life. But it could also mean you want to move and have selected a particular type of house for your move.

For instance, in my early 30s, I was trying to decide whether to stay in San Francisco or move to Santa Monica, and I really liked a particular house near the ocean. But when I called to rent it, I learned it had already been rented, so I thought that was my decision -- move to Santa Monica. I even started packing to go there. However, that night, I dreamt of a house by the ocean, which suggested I should stay in San Francisco after all. So in case that's what I should do, I stayed in San Francisco another day and resumed my search. While I didn't find anything else, later that night the real estate agent for the house I liked called to say the potential renter had backed out of renting the house, so it was mine if I wanted it. And yes, I did. After all, that's what my dream suggested I should do.

But while your wish-fulfillment dreams might be a response to personal wishes, they could also provide ideas for creative projects. For example, just as your dream about flying or traveling to an exotic location might suggest something you would like to do -- whether seeking more freedom or taking a trip, the dream could be a source of new creative possibilities, too. To take the travel dream again, one possibility might be becoming a travel consultant to help clients plan unique trips to less traveled destinations. Or maybe you might design a bag to take on trips or a unique travel guide to exotic locations around the world. In other words, thinking about the content of your dream in new ways can suggest different creative directions, so your dream is not just telling you about yourself, but you are thinking of creative ways to apply your dream content to develop new projects.

Common Meanings in Dreams

As you look to your dreams for meanings to suggest ideas, sometimes your dreams will have symbols that may be meaningful to you, or they may have common meanings that can help you understand your dreams. Most important is what the dream means to you, so use those meanings in interpreting and seeking information from your dreams. But the common meanings for dream images and symbols may resonate with and further inspire you. So I have listed some of the most common symbols that occur in dreams and might trigger your thinking about new ideas. These are drawn from two recent articles about dreams, "58 Most Common Dream Symbols and Their Meaning/Interpretation" from HowtoLucid.com[31] () and "14 Common Dreams and Symbols and Why They're Important" by

---

[31] http://howtolucid.com/dream-interpretation

DreamCloud.³² You might find even more ideas if do a search on Google for "dreams meanings" or "meanings of dreams." You will find dozens of books about dream interpretation on Amazon, too.

Here are some of the common symbols and meanings in these books, along with my thoughts on how a dream symbol might stimulate thinking on how to turn that idea into a creative or profitable project.

Vehicles. These may suggest you are worried about the direction in which you are going in life. A vehicle might also suggest how much control you think you have over whatever path you are on. So a vehicle can help to give you power to make a transition in your life and get to your new destination. Or it can remind you of the obstacles you are facing and the challenges you need to work through.

Alternatively, a dream with one or more vehicles might lead you to look at your car and others' cars to come up with new ideas. For instance, do you find the steering wheel overly cold or hot to

---

³² https://www.huffingtonpost.com/dreams-cloud/meaning-of-dreams_b_4504512.html

touch because of very cold or hot weather? A wool steering wheel cover might be more comfortable to steer with. Or maybe the vehicle in your dream might suggest a plot idea about missing cars due to a burglary ring which is taking cars to Mexico. Then the police find one of the cars with a body in the trunk. And so a best-selling thriller is born. What other ideas do you have if you dream about vehicles?

Being Trapped Someplace. This commonly means you are stuck and need a change or new start. So it may be time for a new job or maybe you need a vacation to relax.

On the other hand, a vivid dream about being trapped might inspire you to think about a new product that helps someone feel un-trapped, such as a way to find lost keys by calling a number on a mobile phone or by clicking a button that triggers a buzzer on your key ring. Or if you're a workshop and seminar leader, maybe a dream of being trapped might suggest a program on how to get unstuck in your life. And as a writer, maybe you might start a novel with people trapped in a cabin by a storm or in a basement by a mad killer, and they have to get out.

Being Chased. Often, if you are chased, this means you are feeling danger or under pressure from something in your life, so it's a signal to look at what is causing your stress. You aren't necessarily running away because you fear being chased in reality, but the dream motif is a wake-up call – for when you are literally awake -- to examine what you are running from in your everyday life that you need to address.

Certainly, that personal problem triggering the chase in your dream could be true. But if you look at this dream in a different way, you may get some ideas. For instance, if you consider what you are running from, maybe this is an experience that others have, too, and you could provide a solution. Say the anxiety is due to bills and taxes. Maybe a solution might be a system that easily organizes everything and even automatically pays selected bills. Or what if the anxiety is related to certain types of people, such as overcharging landlords or school bullies? Maybe create a network of local support groups to research the city laws governing landlords or develop a program to put school bullies into an anti-bullying workshop. Or a book or film might be about how this anti-bullying program works. Or a novel might feature a hero who fights greedy landlords or school bullies.

<u>Encountering Demons, Monsters, or Death</u>. Scary dreams may mean you want to change certain aspects of yourself, particularly if you see yourself as a demon. The dream could inspire you to think about what you don't like about yourself, so you can change that. Or perhaps death can mean that something is ending to make way for something new, or you want a new beginning. Alternatively, maybe the demons or monsters represent real things you are afraid of, while the image of death could represent fear of your own death or that of a loved one, especially if you or they are getting on in years or involved in some risky activity.

Whatever the details, such dreams of demons, monsters, and death can be fertile ground for new ideas, such as the nightmarish dreams that led to classic suspense horror thrillers, like the true story of Frankenstein. Or maybe the demons and monsters might inspire your own version of a children's book, such as in the classic Jack and the Beanstalk tale, where Jack ends up toppling the beanstalk and killing the giant. So what kind of plot does your dream of demons and monsters suggest? Or if you are an artist or jewelry designer, perhaps the images might suggest a painting, sculpture, or jewelry design. Again, think of your dream like a screen with images and story ideas that suggests new directions to take whatever your medium or profession.

<u>Flying.</u> This theme can have different common meanings, depending how high you are flying and whether you encounter any obstacles on your flight. One the one hand, it can be a symbol of being very happy, high, uplifted, and motivated. It can also suggest how much control you feel you have, and whether you feel confident and able to achieve your goals. If you are flying high, great. That means everything is flying along well in your life. But if you are flying low to the ground or get caught in powerlines, that can suggest you are frustrated and need to change something, so you can fly high again.

How do you mine this flying theme for creative project ideas? To take one example for a book or film, what happens during the flight might suggest plot ideas. Where does the flight go? Who are the passengers? Is there any turbulence or other problems on the flight? Could a potential hijacker be on the plane? Maybe a passenger has a panic attack. You get the idea. Try to remember as much as you can for plot ideas. As for a new product or service, maybe you might come up with something for bored travelers, such as a puzzle or novelty item they can play with in their seat or while waiting for their plane to take off or in their seat.

<u>Falling</u>. This is another very common dream motif, closely related to the idea of flying. In fact, they might go together, where you are flying and then fall out of the sky. A common interpretation of the falling theme is that you are considering whether to let go of something you have been holding onto. Or this theme could mean that you keep trying to do something but fail again and again, so it's time to let it go. Or you could feel you are out of control.

Aside from personally using the dream to guide you to let go or regain control, you can consider other creative possibilities. For example, look more closely at the details about falling in your dream. What are you falling from? Where are you falling to? What happens in your fall? Do you feel liberated by doing something new after your fall? Or do you feel you are losing something? And what happens after you land? Such questions may help you find answers for yourself, as well as think about possible future projects. For instance, if the fall is from the air into a forest or other isolated environment, maybe this is like D.B. Cooper's famous fall from an airplane somewhere in the Pacific Northwest that has triggered many stories about what happened to him. These have ranged from living a wealthy charmed life under a new name to falling into a river and being swept away by the current, never to be seen again. Or maybe this falling theme might lead you to think of developing some devices to protect people from injuries from everyday falls, such as slipping on the ice.

Money. A common interpretation is that money represents what you think of your self-worth. So the more money you have in your dream, the higher your self-worth; the less money, the less you think of yourself. Alternatively, maybe the dream is really about the money and having more of it, because money enables you to buy all kinds of things and live a more comfortable life.

Whatever your interpretation, money can get you thinking about different creative outcomes. Look to the details in your dream for ideas about different possibilities. For example, if you lose the money, maybe this can suggest a series of plot twists and turns, as you seek to find out what happened to it. If the money is stolen, maybe this can get you thinking about ways to protect someone from theft or make it easier to file a police report. Or suppose you invest the money. What happens to it? Was it a good investment or bad? In either case, a follow-the-money story can turn into a good detective yarn. Or perhaps you might write about how to invest wisely. Or maybe your dream might inspire a course or workshop on making investment decisions, or it could suggest a new approach to consulting about investments for first time investors.

<u>Being cheated or being late or lost</u>. In this case, a common interpretation is that you feel a lack of trust or security in your relationship or in your ability to prevent yourself from being a victim or getting things done. And sometimes such a dream can be inspired by someone cheating you or by a time when you were late for an appointment or got lost on the road. Sometimes you may experience trying to find your way somewhere, and you continually come to a dead end, which suggests a need to change your path.

But while such a dream is a great reminder to be careful or make changes in yourself, these dreams are especially fertile sources for new ideas. For example, ask yourself more questions about how you were cheated and what you did about it. Notice what you were late for or where you were lost. Even if you can't fill in the details from the dream, see how you might answer these questions in your waking state. For a book or film, imagine how the situation might play itself out for a character in the story. Or perhaps the dream might suggest a book or documentary on how to avoid being cheated or getting lost. As for a new product or service, perhaps people who have been cheated could be helped to get restitution from whoever cheated them. Perhaps you might create a cheat sheet where people could report people who got cheated, such as a local RipOffReport. Or if you are technically inclined, perhaps you could create an app that traces a person's steps, so they can follow them back to where they started to avoid getting lost. Thus, in many ways, you can look into the problems suggested by the dream and think about how to provide solutions.

<u>Hiding from something.</u> Finally, to take one more common dream experience, you might dream about hiding from something or hiding an object from someone. If you are hiding from something, that could be from something real, such as hiding from a criminal or the IRS, or hiding could also represent a fear of some sort of change in your life. If you are hiding an object, it could be a real object you need to protect, such as precious jewelry or favorite pieces of furniture, if you are going through a divorce. Or more generally, the dream could suggest you fear someone taking something you have away from you. In either case, the dream suggests you should look for a resolution, so you don't have to hide or you can protect someone or something from whatever loss you fear.

But the dream could suggest various creative outlets, too. For instance, the plot of a book or film could involve someone hiding away somewhere, such as to avoid retaliation from a criminal mob or government agency. Or the dream might suggest a story about hidden treasure and the search to find it or keep others from finding it. Or the dream could suggest developing some protective products or services to conceal people or objects, such as designer boxes with secret compartments.

Finding Your Own Meanings in Your Dreams

While these common meanings reflect the different images and experiences of a great many dreamers, what is most important is what a dream means to you. Moreover, that meaning can change when you apply the dream to your personal life or think about how the dream suggests ideas for new creative projects or business possibilities. In fact, once you start mining your dreams to inspire new projects and programs, you may have dreams that are more aligned with the information or ideas you are looking for. So the meanings you extract from each dream will change, too.

Thus, as you review each dream, think about what it means for you. It's fine to get insights to help your personal life. But also think about how you might gain new creative projects or directions for your work or business. Then, as you gain insights from what the dream means for you, you can apply them to create these projects or business ideas.

Additionally, you can use these meanings to brainstorm even more ideas, as discussed in the following chapter.

CHAPTER 4: USING YOUR DREAM TO BRAINSTORM NEW IDEAS AND TURN THOSE IDEAS INTO A REALITY

The goal of brainstorming your dreams is to use the ideas, experiences, and any meanings from your dreams to brainstorm further. This way, you use a dream as a starting point to come up with even more ideas, as in any kind of brainstorming session. Then, you review those ideas, decide which ones are useful to turn into reality, and prioritize which ones to further develop. Moreover, as with regular brainstorming, you can do additional brainstorming on any idea that seems promising, so you create a brainstorming tree where you hang more and more ideas like leaves. Then you select the ideas or leaves where you find the most fruit.

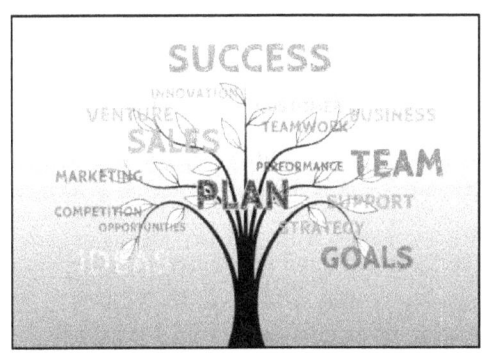 

There are multiple ways to brainstorm -- from brainstorming in writing to drawing as you brainstorm. You can brainstorm individually, with a partner, or in a group. You may already be familiar with at least one type of brainstorming, but I'll review different approaches that apply to working with your dreams. Use whatever approach works best for you. Then, follow the steps for listing your ideas, decide which ones are most workable, and prioritize which ones to implement first and how you will do that.

Beginning the Brainstorming Process

Whatever brainstorming method you use, a first step is selecting the starting point or seed to spark the process. Then, everyone starts watering the seed so it starts to grow.

To select the starting point or seed, choose the idea, experience, or meaning of the dream that most immediately grabs you as something to further think about. Sometimes, it will be very obvious what this is. As you remember or record your dream, something will immediately strike you as the dream's core message or as something to think about further. For example, when I had the dream that led to *Oh Peg It!* I initially saw a track-like board with screws and circles racing around on it, and the vividness of the image led me to want to explore this vision more. So after I woke up, I sketched out this image and vision in the dream and began thinking about what it meant. This then led me to think about the different ways it could become a game, what materials to use in order to play it, what the name of the game might be, and what the cards in the game should say.

I wrote down all of these ideas as I thought of them, so I wouldn't forget them later. Likewise, if something in your dream stands out for you, reflect on this, and write down or record what comes.

What if nothing stands out right away? In that case, you might take more time with the dream to pay attention to what it means or is saying to you. If some insight comes to mind go with that, or if there are multiple insights, write them down, prioritize among them, and brainstorm about that.

On the other hand, if nothing comes to mind after a minute or two of reflection, that's okay, too, because not every dream will have something to say about creative projects or new ideas for your business, just like only some experiences will be memorable among the many experiences you have each day. After all, we live our lives with a multitude of routine daily experiences, but we celebrate the highlights on an occasional basis, for there is no way we could be in a continual mode of celebration. Attempting to do so would turn the process of celebration into a routine experience. Then, we would become like druggies wanting to live in that continual high and seek even higher experiences, until the inevitable overdose of too much drugs or stimulation.

Thus, take a little time to notice your dreams, record them, and notice if there is anything special you can use to get you thinking about further meanings and possibilities, using the brainstorming process. That becomes the seed for these new ideas that come through brainstorming.

You can record information about the dream as soon as you wake up or soon after that, so you remember as much of the dream as possible. Then, you can do the brainstorming later, starting with the content in the dream to get you started.

However you start the brainstorming process -- immediately after you recall the dream or later, using the inspiration of the dream to kick-start the process -- following are different ways to get the most out of your brainstorming.

Different Ways of Brainstorming

The underlying engine of brainstorming is your intuitive or more holistic right brain mind that freely comes up with associations and ideas. Thus, however you brainstorm, let your intuition range freely to generate these ideas. Later, your analytical left-brain mind can review and prioritize them. Initially, you don't want any analytical interference. You just want to come up with ideas you generate freely, without any left-brain censorship.

Whatever type of brainstorming you do, keep a notebook or recording device nearby, so you can quickly write down or record your dream as soon as you wake up. That will help you keep your dream recollections more clearly in mind and help you reduce what you might forget, as your waking consciousness takes over your thoughts.

Following are the major methods of brainstorming. Chose any of them to come up with ideas. Use whatever approach or approaches work best for you. If you need some help getting into the mind-set for brainstorming, I have included some suggestions below. Or refer to a book on brainstorming for more information on using this process.

Write It Down

This is my favorite method of brainstorming, since I've grown up with writing down everything, rather than recording or brainstorming in a group. In this write-it-down method, you furiously write down everything as you think of different ideas. I like handwriting, because I can readily wake up from a dream and start writing quickly in a notebook or on a loose sheet of paper. This way, I feel closer to the dream than if I got up and typed information into a computer, but you can do either -- or start with handwriting and later shift to the computer for even more ideas. Preferably, use a desktop or laptop rather than a mobile device, since typing is usually much slower because of the much smaller keyboard.

In any event, you want to be in a relaxed state, where the ideas come quickly. You may be more likely to be in this state if you write down your ideas by hand while you are still in bed or sitting nearby. Going to a laptop or desk computer to write will often wake you up and disconnect you from your dream, especially since you are likely to associate a laptop or desktop computer with the work you do each day.

Then, taking your seed idea or any idea that has germinated from it, start brainstorming. As ideas come to you, write them down and don't try to judge or evaluate them. That assessment will come in the second stage of the process and if you try to assess the value of the ideas now, that will slow down or stop the idea generation process. So just write, write, write as the ideas come to you. Even if your immediate reaction is the idea is outlandish, it doesn't matter. Write it down. Sometimes even outlandish ideas can contribute to breakthroughs or trigger other valuable ideas, so let whatever comes to you flow in, and write it down.

This approach is much like automatic writing, where you don't think about what you are writing and write down whatever you think. It's a process sometimes used to write memoirs, autobiographies, novels, and other types of material, where free form writing taps into your intuitive mind and you let it flow. The major difference here is that you are starting the process with a specific purpose or objective in mind -- coming up with ideas for creative projects or new business plans.

Should ideas seem repetitious, like you think you thought of something before, just write it down. It could be this is a new idea though it seems similar, or if an idea keeps reoccurring, this could mean the idea is a really good one. So when you evaluate your ideas later, if an idea keeps popping up, that could be a reminder to seriously consider this idea and rank it highly.

Once the ideas start slowing down, you can prod them to continue by asking some relevant or probing questions, such as "Is there anything else?" or "What else might I do?" Stay away from "why" questions, since they tend to slow down the process by asking for an explanation for something that has been suggested, and explanations tend to come from analytical thinking. For now, you are more interested in "what to do" questions to give you some direction on where to go next, not "why" did something happen, a question rooted in the past.

Commonly, at the end of a brainstorming session, your ideas will slow down before they finally stop. So ask your questions during this slowing period, since your mind will be more receptive to continue the process, rather than waiting until the ideas have stopped. That's because it can be harder to start up the brainstorming process, rather than speeding it up, much like having to restart a car after it has stopped, rather than stepping on the gas a little more go a little faster.

Speak It Into a Recording Device

Another brainstorming approach is to speak your ideas into a recording device and listen to them later to review them. Or you might transcribe the recording or have it transcribed, and then review the transcription.

When you speak out your ideas, say them as quickly as you think of them. Don't try to analyze or edit your thoughts as you speak. Just let the ideas flow. If this helps you feel more comfortable, imagine you are talking to someone and sharing your ideas like you are having a conversation with a friend, family member, or associate. Or perhaps imagine you are reporting your experience to a person in authority, such as a teacher, mentor, or religious advisor. Or imagine you are talking to a spiritual being, guide, or wise person in your mind's eye.

In the event that you are making this recording right after you wake up, you can record your thoughts on a computer microphone. If you have a laptop by your bed, this is ideal. Or if you are recording on a desktop, wear whatever you did to bed. Don't try to get dressed, and stay in a relaxed state as long as possible. This way you are more likely to remain in a dreamlike state and better access your dream.

As with writing down your dream, if your thoughts slow down, ask a few probing questions, such as "What else happened?", "What else did I experience?", or "What else do I remember about my dream?" This way you may be able to gain more information and continue the dream process. Keep talking until you run out of things to think about and then stop the recording.

Should you report something that seems familiar, it may be repetitious or it may be a new related idea. So again, don't try to limit, critique, or censor anything you say. Just keep going until you run out of anything to say.

Afterwards, you can play back what you recorded and see if doing so generates any more ideas. If so, turn on the recorder again and record on a different track, so you don't delete anything you previously recorded. Once you are done, you can assess the ideas you have created and determine which ones you like best, so you can prioritize and implement those. Should you find it is hard to do this review process while listening and trying to remember, create a transcript or have your comments transcribed, so you can review them.

Participate in a Group

While brainstorming in a group is a long-established approach for groups to come up with new ideas, this group approach may not be well suited for dreaming, since this is a normally solitary process which occurs at night. But there could be some circumstances where you are in a group and can share productively with each other. Some possibilities might be:

- You are sharing a cabin or tent on a weekend or vacation get-away. In this case, you might try to write quietly in a notebook, binder, or on loose sheets of paper by your bed or a nearby location where you can be alone. Or if you are recording, find a location where you can speak quietly into the recorder without waking anyone.

- You have a dream mentor you can call to share your dream. If so, have a recording device by you or on your phone, so you can record everything.

- You are a member of a dream group, where you are guided into having a dream while at a group event, and thereafter you share your dreams with each other. Sometimes in such a group, you will have some time to write down anything you dream about during the event. Then, you can share what you have written or remember with the group. It is best to write down your thoughts before sharing your insights with others. Or if you are asked to share before writing anything down, bring along your recorder to record what you say. In either case, review your notes or recording transcripts for insights.

Some Ways to Liberate the Creative Process

What if you feel stuck in trying to remember your dream? What sometimes happens is you recall the tail end of the dream or know that you had a dream, but it may not all come back to you right away. In this case, the dream may come back to you if you reflect on it, or sometimes recalling the dream may be triggered by something you see or experience soon after you wake up, such as seeing a picture of someone or something in your dream.

Following are some ways to better remember your dream -- and even recapture a dream that faded away.

Get Into a Relaxed, Meditative State

Often you will be in a relaxed, dreamlike state after you wake up, which is called the "hynopompic" state by dream researchers. It is a mirror state to the "hypnogogic" state, which is the very relaxed dreamlike state you experience between waking and sleeping as you go to sleep. If you are in this state, try to focus your attention on the dream you just had, and sometimes that attention will bring back recollections of your dream, or sometimes you will go back to sleep and continue the dream or have another one.

Ideally, use this relaxed time as you wake up to recall the dream. If you can't do so at this time, say because you are woken up by a phone call or you have an urgent task to do right away, set aside some time as soon as possible after waking to relax and focus on your dream. Recall whatever you can remember and focus on that. Then, if the dream comes back to you, see if any idea or experience inspires you, and brainstorm about that.

Alternatively, if you have made notes about the dream to spur your brainstorming session later, get in a relaxed state whenever you are ready to start brainstorming. There are numerous ways to do this. Here are some of them:

- Sit in a comfortable position on a mat, couch, lounge chair, or other place where you can sit comfortably. Preferably don't lie down, because you may readily fall asleep.

- Be ready to take notes of the ideas that come up or record them as you speak these ideas aloud and pause the device while you are just quietly thinking.
- Close your eyes and repeat certain calming words to yourself, such as "ohmmm."
- Put on some soft calming background music, such the sound of waves, chanting, or slow music.
- Turn off any possible distractions, such as shutting down your cell phone and taking your landline off the hook.
- Put a "Do not disturb" sign on your door.
- If you are not still in your sleepwear, put on some loose, casual clothing.

Once you feel fully relaxed, turn your focus to the subject of your brainstorming and begin.

Speak to a Guide, Teacher, or Wise Person in Your Mind's Eye

Another way to get the brainstorm process going is to speak to a guide, teacher, or wise person in your mind's eye. This being can take any form, from a human to an animal guide to God. As the being appears before you, experience yourself talking to him or her about your dream. As you have a conversation, look for insights and ideas. Then, go through the brainstorming person with that being as your guide or companion with whom you can share anything that comes up for you.

One way to contact such a being is to visualize that person or being before you in whatever form you want. Another method is to go on a journey, where you meet a wise person, often on a mountain top or in a meadow. Or perhaps at the end of this mental journey, you see this teacher or spiritual guide as some kind of animal.

For example, at one time I went on a series of journeys with a guide who led us down through a tree to a lower world where we encountered a deer, lion, eagle, or other animal associated with wisdom for us, and that became our teacher. In other journeys, the guide led us up a tree trunk into the heavens or along a mountain path to a high peak where we met a wise spiritual teacher and could ask a series of questions about ourselves and our direction for the future. More recently, I explored a guided journey with a program called "What's Your Dog Type?" where the teacher took the form of a wise power dog, which could be of any breed.

In any case, whatever form this guide, teacher, or being takes, you can imagine having a conversation in which you brainstorm ideas based on your dream. Having this being there to talk to can help you get your intuitive processes going, so you can come up with even more ideas.

Set Up a Comfortable Environment for Brainstorming

As you work with brainstorming on a regular basis, you may be able to turn on this process almost immediately, wherever you are. I have learned to do this, so wherever I am, if someone asks me a question or I want to come up with ideas for something -- including now, while writing this book -- I let my mind go wherever it will once I have focused on some topic or question. Then, I write down whatever insights I gain from the brainstorming process, so I can later review them to decide which are good to prioritize and pursue and which are not worth any consideration.

Such a comfortable environment can take many forms. It could be a quiet room in your house or a section of a room set up as a special place for brainstorming. Or perhaps you might enhance the specialness of the place with some scented candles, colored lights, or soft music to help you relax and comfortably focus on remembering and then brainstorming about the ideas unleased by your dream.

Begin with a Little Ritual

Sometimes, to help get in the mood for brainstorming, some people use a short ritual to relax and get in the mood. You can similarly do that in brainstorming about your dream ideas.

If you are just waking up and have a dream with ideas you want to remember and learn from, quickly record whatever comes to you. Then, you can use a ritual to transition to brainstorming. If you are still in bed after waking up, you can use a short chant or mentally tell yourself to let your subconscious know you are now brainstorming. For example, chant a simple word, such as "Ohmm" or an inspiring phrase or affirmation, such as "I'm becoming more and more successful through brainstorming."

Another technique is to use some specific actions like a trigger to let your subconscious know that you are ready to start brainstorming. For example, light a candle, wave a feather or other object in the air, or open the pages of your notebook and chant: "Now we can begin. Now we can begin." You can do almost anything that suggests the beginning of a brainstorming session to you. You can also condition yourself, so whenever you engage in these actions or even visualize them in your mind's eye, you can start the brainstorming process as if it's on automatic, because the ritual signals to your unconscious mind that you are ready to begin.

Keeping Track of Your Ideas

Just as you should record your dreams in writing or through an audio recording, you should keep a record of the ideas that you brainstorm in order to later review and assess them. You can make this record in several ways:
- Put your handwritten or typed notes into a binder or loose leaf notebook.
- Have any recordings of your ideas transcribed and put the transcripts into a binder or notebook.
- Create a library or folder on your computer for the files of your recordings and organize them chronologically.

Initially, just create a record, although you can start the assessment process now by starring on paper any ideas you want to pay more attention to later. Or if your ideas are only on a recording, keep a list for each recording, where you note the time and nature of the idea. For instance, if there is a useful idea at 57 seconds, 1 minute and 25 seconds, and at 2 minutes and 15 seconds, note each of these times, and next to each notation add a short phrase to indicate what this idea is about, such as "1:25 - technique for higher ranking on Google; 2:15 - idea for better Facebook ads".

CHAPTER 5: ASSESSING, PRIORITIZING, AND IMPLEMENTING YOUR IDEAS

Once you have generated some ideas from your dream or developed even more from brainstorming, the next step is deciding which ideas have the most merit and thinking how to implement them.

This process of moving from an idea to assessing and implementing it can happen quickly, although I have separated this process into a series of steps. The timeline depends on how rapidly you want to react to your dreams and put them into practice. Sometimes, you might be ready to act immediately; in other cases, you may prefer to let the idea germinate as you think about it from time to time; or sometimes you may put aside some time to actively brainstorm on an idea or series of ideas.

For example, I have had some dream ideas that led to projects I created within the next day or two, such as one time when I dreamt about a man flying on a helicopter commuter service, while I was taking a graduate marketing seminar. We were supposed to come up with an idea for an invented product, and at once I thought this service would be a great idea. So the next day at school, I persuaded my small marketing team to adopt this as our project, and within a day, I created a website for this new service. I called it the "Heliporter," and soon I was laying out the routes for it.

Not only did this "service" prove compelling for the professor, but the website for the service was so realistic that a company which used the name "Heliporters" for airport carts sent me a cease and disaster letter, and it's lawyers came on so strong with their threats of legal action that I ended up getting $4000 to change the name, which I otherwise might have readily changed if they simply asked, since this wasn't a real company.

Today the website for this company under its new name "Heliflyer" still exists as www.heliflyer.org. Additionally, soon after I created the service, the idea for it led to a script for a suspense thriller about a series of mysterious disappearances and murders on the Heliporter commuter service, later changed to the Heliflyers service.

Another way to develop these dream ideas is to take some time to review, assess, and evaluate your initial ideas and the results of brainstorming more ideas. Then, from this larger pool of possibilities, choose what idea or ideas develop. It's a process I've used when I have had several ideas to consider and had to decide which to turn into completed projects.

Following are some ways to engage in this review, assessment, and implementation process. The process is much like goal setting, where you consider different possible goals, prioritize them based on your interests and the practicality of working towards a goal, and lastly take steps to put that goal into practice.

Reviewing and Assessing Your Ideas

Once you have a dream idea that might be worth turning into a creative project or business opportunity, review it to determine if it is practical to develop. If you have a series of dream ideas or have come up with even more ideas from brainstorming, then review, compare, and rate them, so you can choose what's best for you. This process of review and evaluation works much like assessing the value of any ideas, except that these ideas were inspired initially by your dreams. If you already know about this review process, you can skip the following section, though you might still find some useful ideas.

For a Single Idea

Usually, the brainstorming process will generate multiple ideas from your original dream idea. But you can also assess a single dream idea that you think has some merit for a creative project or business program.

To do so, reflect on the idea, but instead of using your more intuitive right-brain mindset, as you would to brainstorm alternatives, review the idea with both your more analytical left-brain mindset and your intuitive abilities to come up with different possibilities. As such, you might do the following to determine how to develop the idea and consider how practical such developments might be.

- Give your idea an overall rating from 1 to 10, based on how strong you think it is. Presumably this rating should be at least a 5 or 6, if you are considering developing the idea.
- Consider the different ways you might develop the idea in different formats, such as turning an idea into a book, film script, workshop series, art piece, new business service, or new product. Then, consider the details to fill in for the particular format you choose. For example, consider the main elements of the plot and the main characters for a novel or screenplay, the main topics to cover in a workshop, what scene to illustrate in a painting, or what specific services to provide to your clients.
- Think about the practicalities of whatever idea you are considering. For example, ask yourself what do you need to do to write the book or script, when can you schedule time to write it, or do you need the help of a ghostwriter to write it for you. Or suppose you are considering a workshop, think about who it is for, how will you get members of the targeted audience to attend. Or say you are thinking of a new product. What do you need to create the prototype? How much will it cost? How will you test the prototype to see that it works? How will you market the project? And so on…

In short, while the initial idea comes from a dream, you still have to consider the value of this idea, just as you would weigh the merits of any other idea from any source.

For Multiple Ideas

When you have multiple ideas from different dreams or from one or more brainstorming sessions, you have to review, assess, and compare them. The process works much like any brainstorming session. You typically rate each idea on the list, usually from 1 to 5. Then, you look at the highest rated ideas. If there is more than one number 1, you further prioritize the highest rated item and drop out the others from further consideration until you have selected the top ranked items to do first, second, and maybe third or fourth. The goal is to choose your favorite idea to implement first, assuming it is practical to do so, and then work on your second and other ideas. The only difference in the process from brainstorming and idea assessment of any type is that you are starting with an idea from a dream.

This process of rating and ranking ideas is a time-tested process you can readily do both individually and in a group, although normally you will be doing dream brainstorming on your own, unless you are part of a dream group that is looking to its members' dreams in deciding what to do. For example, I've been in groups where we all shout out ideas during the brainstorming process. Then, the group leader or group scribe writes down these ideas on a white board for all to see. Next, the group leader asks individuals to vote on their favorite ideas -- sometimes by assigning a 1 to everyone's favorite, a 2 to the next favorite idea, a 3 to the third favorite idea, and so on if the rankings go beyond 3. After that, the group leader adds up the ratings and pulls out the ideas with the most group support, the next most group support, and so on, until there is an ordered list from the most preferred to the ideas at the bottom of the heap. Finally, the favorite idea is the one the group works on first.

Consider your dream ideas in the same way. After you brainstorm ideas inspired by the content in your original dream, go over those ideas and pull out the best ones. Next, determine how practical each one is to implement. Then, think about how to implement those ideas.

Implementing Your New Ideas

Once you have chosen the ideas to turn into creative projects or business opportunities, the final step is implementing them. The process is much like putting into practice your plans for reaching any goal. But this time, you are planning what you need to do to make your dream or brainstormed idea work in real time.

To this end, develop a plan with a series of steps to take and include a timeline for what you are going to do when. If the plan is for a creative project, think of this as an action plan. If you are seeking to increase sales, this becomes a marketing or sales plan. If the objective is the growth of a company and increased profitability, you are developing a business plan.

In short, to implement your new ideas, create a plan for this implementation, which includes the dates and times when you will do something, a detailed description of what you will do, and when you will complete that action described in the plan.

The final step is to actually do it. Now you put your plan into action on a day by day basis, and you monitor the results. This monitoring helps you assess how well the plan is working, so you can, as needed, make changes in order to improve how the plan is operating. If anything isn't working, make changes accordingly. If you need more time to enact parts of the plan, change your timeline as needed. Should you need more help from others to implement the plan, take steps to find that help. Or if someone working on the implementation isn't performing well, replace that person with someone new. Then, should you need further changes to make the plan work, make those changes, too.

If you still need more help in implementing and achieving your goals, there are a great many books on this topic. Just put in "achieving goals," "action plans," or similar terms and you will find dozens of these books. Or bring in a coach or a consultant to help you realize your dreams, in this case, literally! That's because setting and achieving your goals starts with your dreams and the ideas you brainstorm from them. You use these dream-generated ideas to determine your goals for creative projects and business opportunities, and then to determine what you need to do to achieve these goals.

So whatever your ideas, go for it. Turn your dreams into the goals and action plan you have created for realizing your dreams now!

CHAPTER 6: HOW TO DREAM MORE AND INFLUENCE YOUR DREAMS

Want more insights from your dreams? You can get them in several ways:

- Set aside some time when you can go to sleep for a short time and tell yourself to have a dream.
- As you are falling asleep, tell yourself to dream about a particular topic.
- Learn how to access your dreams through lucid dreaming, where you are in a semi-waking state, while you are still dreaming, but you are aware that you are dreaming, so you can guide your dream.
- Create a dream environment that encourages you to have more dreams and more productive ones.

Set Aside Some Time When You Can Go to Sleep and Dream

Aside from going to sleep at the usual time, you can trigger more dreams if you set aside another time or two during the day to go to sleep for a short time. You can combine this method with other techniques for encouraging and directing your dreams.

For example, if there's a suitable area to do this, take about 20 to 40 minutes for a nap in your office. If you have a comfortable chair in your home or office, doze off there. Or if you're at home, go for a nap in the room where you usually go to sleep.

Usually, taking a sleep break once a day is common; though feel free to take a second break, much like some people take a short daily break or two each day for meditation. And sometimes your sleep break may turn into a form of meditation, when you are very relaxed and clear your mind of any thoughts or focus on chanting a word like "ohm." In doing so, you may not sleep but may leave the experience feeling very refreshed and alert. Alternatively, such a meditation break can lead you to fall asleep and dream in this relaxed state.

Sometimes when you want to meditate, you want to avoid falling asleep, so it is best to remain sitting up and even keep your back straight and your feet planted solid on the ground. By contrast, to encourage dreaming, it is best to lie down, because you want to go to sleep. In this case, do whatever you normally do to get in a relaxed, meditative state. But instead of prodding yourself to wake up if you start to fall asleep, you want to drift off to sleep, and commonly, if you fall asleep from a meditative over into a sleep state from a meditative state, you will have an inspiring or comforting dream inspired by your meditation.

If you aren't involved in a regular meditative practice, find a place where you can comfortably go to sleep for about 20 to 40 minutes -- is good for these kinds of naps. Then, besides getting some extra sleep, you will often dream, too.

Encourage Yourself to Dream about a Particular Topic

You can actually shape your dreams, if you direct your thoughts before you go to sleep to what you want to dream about. To do this, think about your goal for a dream before you go to sleep.

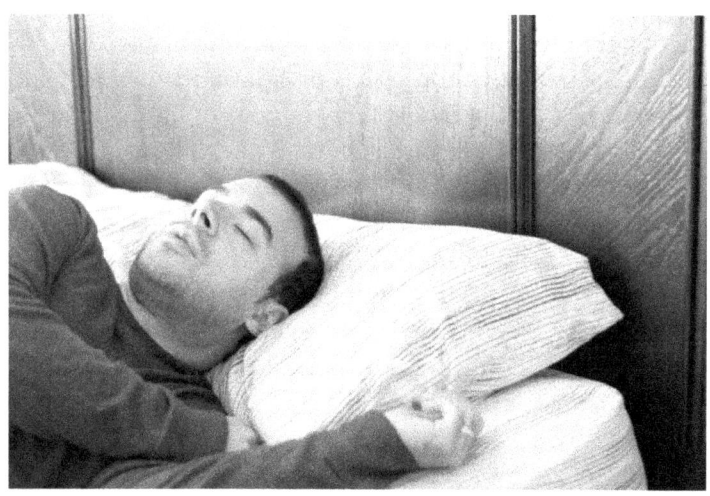

You don't want to think too actively, which will interfere with falling asleep as the thoughts race around your head. Thus, don't think about a problem and come up with alternatives and solutions, which can keep you actively thinking as you try to solve the problem. This is also not the time to play out multiple responses, if you are angry at someone about something. Such thinking can add fuel to your anger and keep you awake thinking about how to best respond.

Instead, think about what you want to dream about in general terms. For example, make a statement or ask a question, and turn that over to your unconscious or subconscious mind to come up with responses. Or perhaps focus on a word, phrase, question, or image you associate with whatever you want to dream about.

For example, if you want to come up ideas for a plot in a novel or film script, you might ask a question like: "What happens to Frankie after he gets to the cabin?" But don't try to answer this question mentally. Instead, focus on the question or repeat it again and again as you are in this very relaxed pre-sleep hypnogogic state. Or suppose you are thinking about a new product or invention. You might ask about the problem you are trying to solve. Or you might imagine a prototype on the mental screen in your head. Then, your question might be: "What can this product/invention do to help people?" You might focus on the prototype and see what happens to it in your dream.

This kind of pre-dream warm-up will help you go into your dream with your attention focused on what you want to dream about. Then, this focus will help to trigger a dream on that subject and sometimes provide you with answers to the problems you are trying to solve. Or a dream might also suggest a new idea to develop.

Does this approach really work, you might wonder, since people don't normally think about structuring what to dream about in advance. They think a dream just happens. But now, a number of dream experts have suggestions for specific steps to guide the process. Plus, you can combine these techniques for direct control with lucid dreaming to further direct the dream while it is going on. Also, have a dream journal or paper ready when you wake up, so you can record what you experience, since we are more likely to remember our last dream, though we may have several dreams when asleep.

For example, Anna LeMind, the founder and lead editor of Learning-mind.com, who writes about science, psychology, and consciousness, suggests these 10 steps to program your dreams, so you dream about what you want to dream about.[33] Here and there I have expanded on her 10 steps.

1. A few hours before you go to bed, try to relax and avoid having unnecessary emotions and experiences, and don't have a heavy meal or engage in extensive physical exercise.

2. Decide on what you want to dream about, though don't provide a detailed description, since dreams play out through their own internal logic. Rather, specify the type of intellectual or creative problem you want to solve, which could relate to a personal concern or a creative project.

3. Write down the purpose of the dream you hope to program.

---

[33] Anna LeMind, "10 Steps to Programming our Dreams," https://www.learning-mind.com/10-steps-to-programming-your-dreams

4. Get ready to remember your dream by putting down something to write on next to your bed, so you can write down as many details as possible after you wake up.

5. Program yourself to wake up as soon as you dream what you want to dream about, so you can remember it, rather than having it disappear as other dreams occur. To program yourself in this way, you might tell yourself before going to sleep that you will wake up as soon as you have the desired dream.

6. Learn how to enter the altered state of consciousness you experience before or after you go to sleep, which are the hypnogogic and hypnopompic states. To stay in this altered state, don't fall asleep immediately when you lie down or jump out of bed as soon as you wake up. Seek to stay in this state between your dream and everyday reality, because this is like a "window to the worlds where we can get important information."

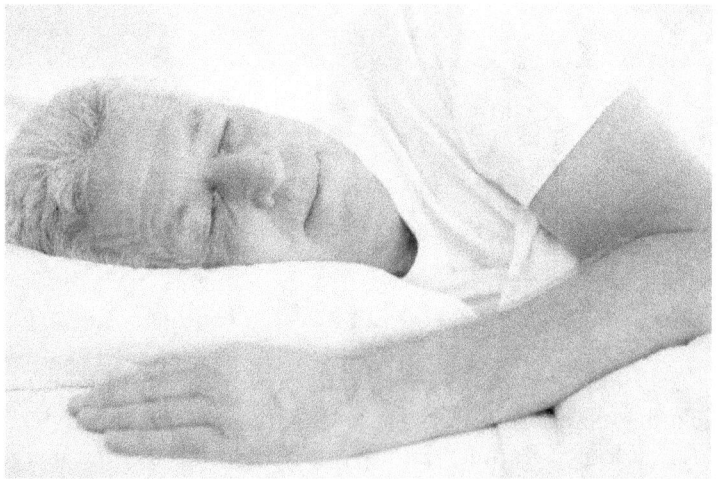

7. While in this altered state of consciousness as you fall asleep, visualize the subject you want to dream about by seeing an image or imagine the thought like a text in your mind.

8. Once you wake up, don't immediately seek to return to everyday reality. Instead, try to hold onto the bits of pictures or recollections from your dream that you can still recall.

9. Once you are fully awake, write down everything you remember and whatever else you think about before you get out of bed. (And as previously noted, you can use a recorder to record your thoughts).

10. Through this deliberate approach to dream programming, you should be able to dream about what you want, and these dreams can help you personally and in coming up with creative and productive ideas.

This approach for conscious dreaming is similarly recommended by Erin Pavlina, an intuitive counselor who helps clients gain spiritual insights that help them in everyday life. As she sums up this approach for using lucid dreaming to guide your programmed dreams:

> "Lay down while you're tired but make sure you can stay awake for at least 10 minutes or so before drifting off. Now literally think and daydream the dream you want to have. Let it play out in your mind…The more times you can let the scene play out in your mind before you fall asleep, the better. It's best to do this while you are tired. Keep thinking of the scene and characters as you fall sleep. Don't start thinking about your morning's to do list or how you're going to avoid (a particular problem). Just keep your conscious mind on the dream images you want to have."

Use Lucid Dreaming to Guide Your Dream

Another technique which can be a little harder to master is using lucid dreaming to influence the content of your dream. A lucid dream occurs when you are still dreaming but are aware of the dreaming. This can occur when you are having a normal dream and suddenly realize you are dreaming -- a "dream-initiated lucid dream." Or you can experience a "wake-initiated lucid dream," when you go from a normal waking state into a dream, but remain aware you are dreaming.

This lucid dreaming technique can take some training, but it really does work -- and you can learn to induce such a dream as I experienced many years ago in the 1990s, when I was at a workshop on lucid dreaming at Esalen, a center in Big Sur devoted to personal growth experiences. Founded it 1962 by Michael Murphy and Dick Price, Esalen is considered by many to be the birthplace of the human potential movement, and it still exists. In the workshop, we were taught one of the techniques to induce a lucid dream -- telling yourself before falling asleep that you will remain aware you are dreaming. Then, once you have a dream, you can tell it what to do, and the dream will continue as you observe it. I don't remember exactly what my dream was about anymore, but I remember having that experience and discussing it with other attendees who similarly experienced that phenomenon.

Afterwards, I wasn't able to consciously induce such a directed dream, and over time, I stopped trying, though occasionally I had a lucid dream, where I knew I was dreaming and observed it like watching a movie, but I didn't try to direct it. So it is possible to have this experience, and if you want to use it to guide a creative project or develop a business opportunity, you can do it.

The idea of lucid dreaming has a long history, which helps to show it works. Back in ancient Greece, the philosopher Aristotle pointed out that "often when one is asleep, there is something in consciousness which declares that what then presents itself is but a dream." The physician Galen even used lucid dreams for therapy. And the Tibetans developed a practice of dream Yoga, based on a dreamer remaining aware that he or she was dreaming.[34]

Later, in the 17th century, the philosopher and physician Sir Thomas Brown described his ability to use a lucid dream for creative endeavors in the *Religio Medici*. As he wrote: "In one dream I can compose a whole Comedy, behold the action, apprehend the jests and laugh myself awake at the conceits thereof."

Then, in the 19th century, in 1867, a scholar of China, Marie-Jean-Leon, described his experiences of lucid dreams in a book: *Les Reves at Les Moyens de Les Diriger: Observations Pratiques*, which translates into *"Dreams and the Ways to Direct Them; Practical Observations."* In his view, anyone can learn to dream consciously.

---

[34]"Lucid Dream," Widipedia, https://en.wikipedia.org/wiki/Lucid_dream.

In fact, recent research by neuroscientists has suggested that conscious dreaming is a unique state of consciousness associated with REM -- rapid eye movement – sleep. In other research between 1982 and 2006, neuroscientist J. Allan Hobson explored the brain activity during lucid dreaming. Among other things, he, like other researchers, found that lucid dreams begin in the REM stage of sleep, and he found that there was more of a beta-1 frequency of brain activity (from 13-19 Hz) for lucid dreams. In turn, this increased activity in the parietal lobes made lucid dreaming a conscious process.[35]

In a 2009 study at the Neurological Laboratory in Frankfort, researchers found even more brain activity during lucid dreams. They found an EEG (electroencephalogram) recorded brainwave frequencies of up to 40 HZ during a lucid dream. The researchers also found more activity in the frontal and frontolateral areas of the brain, which are the seat of linguistic thought and other higher mental functions linked to awareness. So you aren't just imagining this conscious dreaming experience -- it is very real. In fact, a study from Frankfurt University in 2014 found that lucid dreams can be induced by electrically stimulating the brain of sleeping individuals with harmless 30-second jolts of electrical current to the frontal cortex. Before they had had non-lucid dreams, but now the subjects reported that they had vivid dreams in which they recognized they were dreaming. In fact, 77% of the time, the stimulation at 40 Hz worked.[36] So down the road, perhaps, there could be places where you could go to stimulate your dreams.

How do you control your dreams? The basic process involves thinking of what you dream about, much like pre-programming your dreams and later remembering them. The key is that you are conscious of what you are dreaming about it, and you sometimes can insert your consciousness into your dream, so you may be able to exert some control over what happens in the dream, while you continue dreaming.

---

[35]"Lucid Dream."
[36]"World of Lucid Dreaming: Learn How to Control Your Dreams," Wikihow. http://www.world-of-lucid-dreaming.com

Some of the techniques for exercising this control include the following:

- Remind yourself to be aware when you are dreaming before you go to sleep. For example, you might repeat a phrase to yourself such as "I will be aware that I'm dreaming," or "I will know I'm dreaming," as you fall asleep. The technique is called "Mnemonic Induction to Lucid Dreaming" or MILD, which involves using a memory aid, in this case a phrase, to turn your dreaming into an automatic habit.[37]

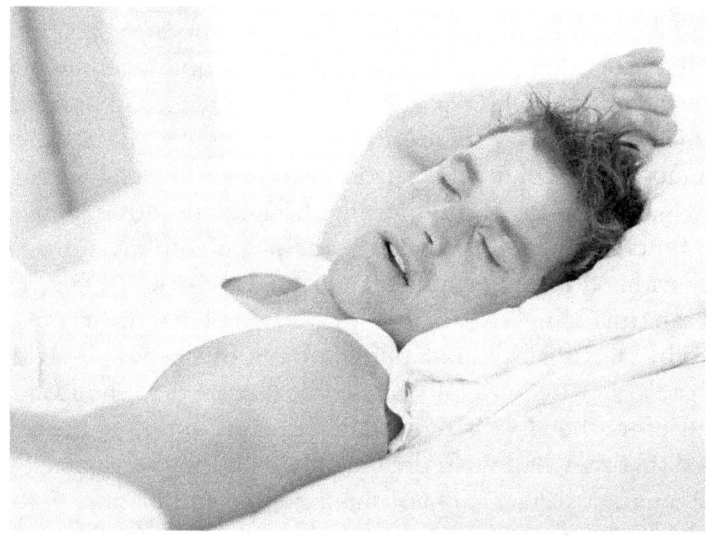

- After you wake up from a dream -- which you ideally write down or record -- close your eyes and focus on the dream. Then, imagine that you were in the dream and recognize it as a dream. Hold onto this thought as you drift back to sleep. That thinking might trigger a lucid dream, whereas most lucid dreams occur when someone is fully asleep, notices an unusual event, and realizes he or she is in a dream.

- Wake yourself up in the middle of the night by setting an alarm to go off 4, 5, 6, or 7 hours after you fall asleep, since you are more likely to be in REM sleep at these times. However, setting it

---

[37]"How to Lucid Dream," Wikihow. (https://www.wikihow.com/Lucid-Dream

for 6 or 7 hours is more likely to produce lucid dreams, since these later REM phases last longer.

- Meditate in a quiet, dark room before you go to sleep and initially pay attention to your breathing, imagine going up and down stairs, or do anything else to get very relaxed and comfortable, so you slip into a wake-induced lucid dream. Although such dreams are less likely than a dream-induced lucid dream, you can still trigger them in this way.

- Take some of the drugs designed to induce lucid dreams, such as galantamine, a drug synthesized from the snowdrop plant.[38] Or take one of the assorted dream herbs, pills, and supplements that have been developed to make your lucid dreams more clear and vivid, such as Claridream PRO, which is a blend of Chinese club moss, valerian root, passion flower, and chamomile.[39]

As to how to guide your dream, once in this lucid state, that can be something to work on programming in advance, just as you might give yourself suggestions before you go to sleep on what to dream about. Likewise, you can apply these suggestions to exert some control over the characters, events, or settings of your dream, from guiding plot ideas and developing creative designs to coming up with ideas for your business. This dream programming takes some training and practice, and a number of courses will help you learn how to do this. Just Google "Lucid dreams," and you can research different programs and decide if one is right for you.

Create a Dream Environment that Encourages You to Have More Dreams -- and More Productive Ones

Creating a receptive dream environment can help you have lucid dreams, too. Just as this environment can facilitate dreams generally, so it can be used to direct your dreams while you are having them.

---

[38] "How to Lucid Dream."
[39] "World of Lucid Dreaming."

Moreover, you might set up the environment to stimulate particular dreams, such as if you put up posters with images that relate to the topic you want to dream about. For example, if you are working up a novel or script about a mysterious person dressed in black, put up illustrations or photos with a person wearing black. If you have an idea for a business involving solar panels, put up illustrations of panels on a roof.

In choosing an environment for dreaming, ideally have a place set aside for this purpose, such as a room in your house or office, where you can quickly set up any devices you use to stimulate or record your dreams. Preferably, lock the door during the time for sleeping and dreaming, so you won't be disturbed. If you think someone might come by, put up a "Do Not Disturb" sign. Also, it is ideal if you have a bed or couch, so you can fully recline. Alternatively, roll out a mat for the floor or use a lounge chair. You can, of course, use your own bedroom for the times when you hope to inspire lucid dreams apart from encouraging these dreams at night. But it can be ideal to have an additional place to retreat to, like having a second vacation home.

In turn, having this special place can help to trigger dreams through the magic of conditioning. As you repeatedly go to this place to have a lucid dream, you create a habit of doing this, so after a time, just going there -- or even thinking about going there in a relaxed state -- can trigger a dream.

Such an environment can be set up like any place you might use to relax and fall asleep. For example, this setting might include some incense, candles, low or no lighting, extra heating, some blankets, and soft music. Additionally, you might have a recording with a repeating phrase to remind you to remain aware of your dream or the content you want to dream about.

To illustrate, the recording might repeat the words:
- "I will remember my dream….I will remember my dream,"
- "I will be aware when I am dreaming…I will be aware when I am dreaming,"
- "I will stay in control of my dream and direct what I am dreaming…I will stay in control of my dream and direct what I am dreaming."

Or to focus on what you are dreaming about, the recording might repeat these words:

- "My dream will be about_____... My dream will be about _____."
- "I will dream about_____ I will dream about_____."

Try experimenting with what works best for you. It may be better to separate the recordings about the process of dreaming from the recordings about content, so your focus is on one thing at a time when you are stimulating a dream. Or you might alternate the messages and see how that works. For example, one message might be about how you will remember, be aware of, or stay in control of your dream. Another message might be what you want to dream about, so you can get ideas from your dream for your creative project.

Drawing Insights from Other Types of Dreaming or Dreamlike States

Besides gaining insights from remembering or influencing your dreams when asleep, you can gain insights from other dreamlike states, which include daydreaming, relaxing, meditating, and hypnosis. Ideally, have something to write or record on readily available should you get ideas from any of these activities.

Daydreaming

Daydreaming can occur at any time. Your mind just wanders off, stimulated by something dull that you aren't interested in or by something that catches your fancy while you are doing something else. I've had this experience many times, especially at a meeting or presentation where a not-very good speaker drones on. So daydreaming serves as an escape valve. Suddenly, my mind is miles away, traveling somewhere more interesting -- whether I'm at a different place like a tropical island or thinking about what I'm going to do next and planning that project.

When a daydream happens, you often notice you are daydreaming and quickly pull your attention back to whatever you are doing. If you can, you might go into a mental reverse to recapture what you missed, such as when you are watching a video or TV program. For instance, sometimes late at night, while I'm watching a movie on Netflix, my attention wanders and suddenly I'm thinking about something else. But I notice my thoughts are elsewhere, so I snap back. Then, I rewind the program a few scenes to where my mind drifted off and I continue the program from there.

This kind of minor mental lapse can occur from time to time, and each time, you might become quickly aware that your mind has wandered and return your attention to what you were observing before. You can also use this moment when you become conscious of your daydream to write down or record anything useful. Additionally, whether you write or record anything, you can use this moment to guide your daydream.

Relaxing

Sometimes relaxing can trigger different types of dreams –
- A regular dream, since you have drifted off to sleep;
- A lucid dream, where you are aware you are dreaming and can exercise control if you want;
- A daydream, where your mind is drifting in a hazy state between waking and sleeping.

In this case, you can let your mind continue to drift where it will and simply observe. Or if you prefer, mentally steer your dreaming in the direction you want to gain ideas. Then, if any ideas are useful, write them down or record them.

You can also take time to relax and pay attention to whatever you are thinking about at the time. You can do this in any number of situations -- as you lounge on a beach chair by the pool, relax by the fire on a ski trip, go camping in the mountains, watch a baseball game, or sit on a couch listening to music. In other words, you can relax doing almost anything, as long as you like doing it and find it relaxing. Then, being very relaxed can trigger any of these dream states, where you can observe or take some action to guide your dream.

Meditating

Meditating can also trigger your thoughts. A common goal of meditating is to clear your mind of any distracting thoughts or environmental input, so you can focus on a word "like om" and silently say or chant that word again and again. Or you might meditate during some yoga practice, such as assuming a posture like squatting on your legs or raising your arms up and down.

Whatever type of meditation you practice, you can use the meditative state as a jumping off point to trigger different types of dreams, based on whether you want to observe or guide your dreaming. Or you can let the meditative experience guide you, so you are open to whatever comes -- whether it's a memory, association, word, or dream. Then, whatever form the dream experience takes, be ready to remember what you can and take notes or make a recording, so you can capture any ideas for later use.

Alternatively, you can direct your meditation to focus on coming up with ideas, plans, or whatever else you want to imagine. Aside from considering what to do next, you can use meditation to come up with plans and imagine how to implement those plans. If you do so, your meditation can lead to intuitive brainstorming, where you see images as well as thoughts come to mind and you see them happening in the here and now. For example, I have used this approach to come up with the steps of what to do to turn some ideas into a practical project.

Hypnosis

Finally, you can use hypnosis to come up with ideas. Here you take a more active role yourself or with the help of a hypnotist to focus on generating ideas for a particular purpose. You get into a hypnotic state in which you try to see these ideas come to life as thoughts or images -- and you can take notes after the experience or record what you are seeing in your mind's eye.

To get into this state, you can work with a hypnotist or use a recording with an induction to guide you, such as with the following words spoken softly and soothingly: "You are paying attention to your breathing, and as you breathe in and out, you are feeling more and more relaxed, more and more relaxed, and you are going deeper, deeper into this very relaxed state."). Then, once you are in this state, the hypnotist or recording will provide some directions to guide your journey.

For instance, the words on the recording or spoken by the hypnotist might take you on a journey after which you get answers to questions or see images of what you are seeking. This process could even take the form of a shamanic journey, where you go to meet a wise man or woman who will have some answers for you in response to your question. In one of my experiences, a friend guided me down an elevator to the basement of Macy's where I saw all kinds of toys. In another case, I went on a series of shamanic and other journeys at Esalen where I began each journey with a question, such as "What do I most want to do in the coming year?" Then I saw some answers. I also had several hypnosis sessions with a hypnotist who guided me to imagine a series of stories I could use to create some children's books -- and after several sessions, I turned a half-dozen of these stories into picture books for kids.

A good way to use this state to come up with ideas for your projects or business is to start with a question or statement about the information you are seeking. For instance, you might ask:
- "What should my next book or script be about?"
- "What can I do to increase my business?"
- "What new products or services can I add over the next few months"
- "I'd like to know what I should write about/design next."
- "I'd like to know how to solve this problem I'm facing at work (and state the problem you want to resolve).

Then, with this question or statement in mind, get into the hypnotic state with the help of a recording or hypnotist to guide you. Once you are in this deeply relaxed state, let your mind go so the ideas come to you. Don't try to direct them. Just relax and let your intuitive mind take over to send the ideas to you. At the end of the experience, use a reverse count or other method to return to ordinary consciousness. This reverse count might go something like this: "Okay, now I'm going to count backwards from 5 to 1 and as I do, you will become more and more awake -- 5, 4... Becoming more and more awake... 3, even more awake... 2, you're almost back, and 1, now you can open your eyes and come back into the room."

While in this state, you can describe what you are experiencing aloud and record what you say and listen back or later transcribe your statements. Or you can write down or record your recollections of your experience immediately after you return from the hypnotic state.

Summing Up

In short, there are a number of ways to get ideas for your creative projects or business apart from having regular dreams and remembering them. These methods include programming your dreams, having lucid dreams, daydreaming, relaxing, meditating, and hypnosis.

Use any approaches or combination of approaches that work for you. Whatever approaches you choose, make a record of what you experience in writing or in a recording which you later listen to or transcribe. Then, decide which ideas are most useful, prioritize those you want to use, and create an action plan to put those ideas into practice. The final step is to implement that plan.

These different dreaming techniques are thus a source of the ideas and insights. Then, you need to review and assess them and make the most useful ideas actually happen.

CHAPTER 7: TURN YOUR DREAM IDEAS INTO A NEW BOOK OR PROJECT

Now you have got your idea and have selected and prioritized your ideas, as discussed in Chapter 5. Next, for each idea, engage in a series of steps to turn that into a completed and profitable project. Doing so is much like going from any goal or idea to a finished project, which is the topic of many books and workshops. And you may already be engaging in this process with other creative projects or business ideas. So I'll only briefly cover the steps to implementing and making your ideas real briefly.

For a Book

1) Determine who the book is for and why they would be interested in your book.
2) Brainstorm or list all the topics you want to cover in your book, keeping your target audience and their reasons for being interested in mind.
3) Combine any related topics together.
4) Organize the topic list into the order in which you want to cover each topic.
5) Create an outline for your book from this list.
6) Turn your outline into a series of chapters.
   - Aim for 8-12 chapters.
   - If there are too many chapters, combine items in your outline together into a chapter.
   - If there are not enough chapters, break up some chapters to create more chapters.
7) Divide each chapter into sections, based on topics or incidents
8) Write up one or more sections each day, spending about 1-3 hours writing them.
   - Ideally, devote at least 3 days a week to this process.
   - Figure on writing about 2 to 3 pages of about 250-300 words each per hour

9) Ideally, your book should be at least 40-100 pages for a self-published book (10,000- 25,000 words) and 150-300 pages for a book with a traditional publisher (50,000-90,000 words).
10) Edit and polish your book, add any illustrations, and you are done.
11) Now market, promote, and sell your book.

For a Creative Project or New Business Idea

1) Determine the market for this new project or business idea and why readers might want it.
2) Do some market testing to determine if this is the correct market, the main reasons individuals are interested in this idea or business, and how to best let them know about this new project or business idea.
3) Create a prototype or pilot program for this new project or business idea.
4) Write up a project plan or business plan for how you will create or launch this business.
5) List the steps to implement the plan.
6) Create a timeline for when you will undertake each step.
7) Turn that timeline into action.
8) If needed, raise money for your project or business idea using your prototype or plan to help you in obtaining the needed funds, using whatever method is best for your project (from crowdfunding to getting equity capital to obtaining a loan)
9) Market, sell, and promote your product, service, or business idea.
10) Be ready to modify your idea for your project or business or your plan for implementing it, if you get any negative feedback.
11) Assess any negative feedback to determine what modifications to make, if any.
12) If your project or business idea gains growing interest, expand your promotion, develop more projects, or find ways to grow your business even more.

The way to follow these steps will depend on your project, resources, the number of people involved, and other factors. Accordingly, get a book or books or participate in a seminar or workshop on developing and promoting whatever you are doing. Additionally, consider working with a coach or consultant who can guide you personally on turning your idea into a completed book, product, service, or business, and then market, promote, and sell whatever you develop. Based on what you need, you can hire communications, marketing, promotion, sales, financial and other types of coaches and consults.

So now, get going. Turn your ideas into successfully achieving your goal. Then, use this same process to come up with even more ideas to develop in the future.

CHAPTER 8: CREATING A SUPPORT GROUP TO ENCOURAGE AND NUTURE YOUR DREAMS

Once you find the process of developing ideas from your dreams helpful, consider creating a group of others who are similarly getting ideas from their dreams or interested in learning how to do this. You might use this as a mastermind group to help one another in getting ideas, choosing which ideas to develop, or actually developing them.

Here are some ways to start such a group. I will only briefly suggest such ideas, since there are all kinds of articles and books on how to create and work with a support or mastermind group. Some ways to create such a group are the following:

1) <u>Develop a plan for what you want this group to do</u>. Is it a support group, a mastermind group, a group to talk about techniques for dreaming, a group to help brainstorm and select ideas to develop? Or maybe the group can be a combination of these things. You can talk about the focus of the group in your first meeting.

2) <u>Create an invitation to let others know about joining the group</u>. This copy can take the form of an announcement to a business referral group, a listing on an online community forum, a notice on a local Craigslist or a posting on Facebook, LinkedIn, Twitter, or other social media.

3) <u>Organize your first meeting</u>. One ideal place for setting up a local interest group is Meetup at www.meetup.com. You decide what the group is about, give it a name, write up some copy to describe it and yourself, indicate up to 15 types of interests that potential members might have, decide on a date for your meeting -- generally about 2 or 3 weeks after your announcement, and describe your revent in an appealing way. Figure on about 1 ½ to 2 ½ hours for your first meeting. Meetup will send out an announcement about your group a

day or two after you create it, and if your meeting is already set up, people will RSVP. Alternatively, make arrangements with groups where you are a member to host your meeting, such as if you belong to a co-working group, church group, of special interest group.

4) Promote your meeting. Actively let people know about your first meeting. Apart from anything Meetup or your host group does, you can post announcements on Facebook, LinkedIn, Twitter, and Instagram. You can also make an announcement on your online community forum, Craigslist, or on the social media, much as you might do in forming the group. But now you are promoting your first meeting.

5) Get set up for your meeting. These arrangements might involve creating an agenda and printing copies for attendees, preparing refreshments, and setting up the room and any audiovisual equipment, such as for a PowerPoint presentation. You might also review what you plan to say at the meeting, such as describing your plan for the group, inviting introductions, leading a discussion about the dream ideas participants have had, and offering advice on developing these ideas.

6) Conduct your meeting. Now facilitate the meeting. A good format for these meetings is:
- about 15-20 minutes for arrivals and networking;
- about 10-15 minutes for introductions where people talk about what they do in the real world, why they are interested in this group, and their experience with using dreams for ideas;
- about 5-10 minutes to introduce yourself, your reasons for starting the group, what you hope to do at meetings, and what people would like gain from attending;
- about 20-30 minutes for people to share on the ideas they have gotten from dreams and what they would to do with their ideas, and how the group might help them develop their ideas;
- about 30-60 minutes to brainstorm ways to develop ideas, share advice, or mastermind ideas for developing, implementing, and promoting ideas;

- about 15-20 minutes to conclude the meeting by talking about what people would like to do at the next meeting followed by additional time for networking and informal conversation. If there is interest, you might suggest that some of you could get together to experiment with different dreaming techniques to get ideas.

So happy dreaming on your own or in a group! And may your dreams lead to great new ideas in the future.

ABOUT THE AUTHOR

GINI GRAHAM SCOTT, Ph.D., J.D., is a nationally known writer, consultant, speaker, and seminar leader, specializing in business and work relationships, professional and personal development, social trends, and popular culture. She has published over 50 books with major publishers. She has worked with dozens of clients on memoirs, self-help, popular business books, and film scripts. Writing samples are at www.changemakerspublishingandwriting.com. She has been a Huffington Post columnist, commenting on social trends, business, and everyday life at www.huffingtonpost.com/gini-graham-scott.

She is the founder of Changemakers Publishing, featuring books on work, business, psychology, social trends, and self-help. It has published over 100 print, e-books, and audiobooks. She has licensed several dozen books for foreign sales, including the UK, Russia, Korea, Spain, and Japan.

She has received national media exposure for her books, including appearances on *Good Morning America*, *Oprah*, and *CNN*. She has been the producer and host of a talk show series, *Changemakers*, featuring interviews on social trends.

Her books on success in professional and personal development include:
Self-Publishing Secrets
Self-Publish Your Book in Multiple Formats
Turn Your Dreams into Reality
Mind Power: Picture Your Way to Success in Business
Resolving Conflict

Scott is active in a number of community and business groups, including the Lafayette, Pleasant Hill, and Danville Chambers of Commerce. She is a graduate of the prestigious Leadership Contra Costa program, is a member of two B2B groups in Danville and

Walnut Creek, and a BNI member. She does workshops and seminars on the topics of her books.

She received her Ph.D. from the University of California, Berkeley, and her J.D. from the University of San Francisco Law School. She has received five MAs at Cal State University, East Bay.

CHANGEMAKERS PUBLISHING
3527 Mt. Diablo Blvd., #273
Lafayette, CA 94549
changemakers@pacbell.net . (925) 385-0608
www.changemakerspublishingandwriting.com

www.ingramcontent.com/pod-product-compliance
Lightning Source LLC
Chambersburg PA
CBHW071530080526
44588CB00011B/1631